QUOTES AND WORDS OF INSPIRATION

Published by Brolga Publishing Pty Ltd 2010
PO Box 12544 A'Beckett St Melbourne Australia 8006
ABN 46 063 962 443
email: sales@brolgapublishing.com.au
web: www.brolgapublishing.com.au

All rights reserved. No part of this publication may be reproduced, stored in a retrieval system or transmitted in any form or by any means electronic, mechanical, photocopying, recording or otherwise without prior permission from the publisher.

Copyright 2010 © George Norris

National Library of Australia Cataloguing-in-Publication entry
    Norris, George D., 1940-
    Quotes and words of inspiration
    9781921596452 (pbk.)
    Inspiration–Quotations, maxims, etc.
    Success–Quotations, maxims, etc.
    Wisdom–Quotations, maxims, etc.
    Motivation (Psychology)–Quotations, maxims, etc.
    158.1

Printed in Indonesia
Cover design by David Khan
Typesetting by Esther van Doornum

QUOTES AND WORDS OF INSPIRATION

strategies for success for every day of the year

George Norris

Foreword

Lots of people have suggested to me over the years that they have a great idea for a radio segment, but become disillusioned very quickly when it's pointed out they need to come up with a new topic every day, possibly for years.

That means two things: It's a lot of very hard work, and you better know what you're talking about. When George and I first met at the suggestion of a mutual friend, George had in mind a weekly segment, but when I told him I'd like a daily segment he didn't flinch for a moment, despite being well aware of the daunting requirements.

We chatted in that first meeting for quite some time, helped along no end by our mutual love of golf. It became glaringly obvious that George was not only an engaging person, but a very professional communicator who could bring something unique to our radio station.

George wasn't all that thrilled when I wanted to call his segment "The Life Coach" because many lesser and less qualified individuals had tapped into that title to peddle their ideas, and of course George's business experience and cliental also extended way beyond that of the average "Life Coach".

But George accepted my argument that we needed a short, snappy and easily identifiable moniker for our radio listeners to grasp (thanks George), and so his daily segment came to life.

The segment has now run continuously for some five years, and it says much about George's professionalism, dedication and work ethic, that he continues to churn out fresh material every day, and does so with boundless enthusiasm and optimism for the future.

Personally, I have also come to know George as a friend and someone I enjoy being in the company of. And whenever we talk, golf of course still enters the conversation somewhere.

Gary Hoffman
Station Manager, Radio Magic 1278

DYLAN THOMAS
WELSH POET AND WRITER

**"Do not go gentle into that good night.
Old age should burn and rage at close of day."**

If this applies to you, it's important to realise that if you continue learning and striving to achieve, you will stay young and vibrant.

However, it's up to you. If you think you're old, you'll become old, tired, lazy and depressed; but if you continue to learn, and keep your mind active and open, you will remain young and in-tune with the ever changing world around you.

Remember, age is just a number not a condition so think young and live your dreams.

JOHN STEINBECK
AMERICAN NOVELIST

"No-one wants advice – only corroboration."

How true, but it also reminds me of a well-known proverb, "The way of a fool seems right to him, but a wise man listens to advice".

Therefore, before you take a leap into the unknown take heed of advice and your life's journey will be a smoother ride and your destination more achievable.

Remember, we have two ears and only one mouth, so listen twice as much as you talk and gain wisdom.

HENRY DAVID THOREAU
AMERICAN ESSAYIST AND POET

"Things do not change – we change."

In other words, it is up to you to make changes in your life. Remember, determination, patience and courage are the only things needed to improve any situation, and if you want a situation changed badly enough, you will need to find these three attributes.

So if "change" is your new year's resolution, don't just say you want to change. If you want it badly enough it is up to you to take action, make a list of goals you want to achieve and as they say,
"Just do it".

WILLIAM JAMES
AMERICAN PSYCHOLOGIST AND PHILOSOPHER

"Keep the faculty of effort alive in you by a little gratuitous exercise every day. That is be systematically heroic in little unnecessary points, do every day or two something for no other reason than it's difficult."

What that means in simple terms is, challenge yourself regularly. You will find it easier to cope with the difficulties of life and it will become easier. The hurdles will become smaller, life will become more manageable and you will gain confidence by being more in control of yourself.

BENJAMIN FRANKLIN
AMERICAN PRESIDENT, STATESMAN AND PHILOSOPHER

"He that is good at making excuses is seldom good at anything else."

So, take responsibility for yourself, admit and come to terms with your errors and limitations, build on your strengths and work on improving your weaknesses. We all make mistakes and we all have gifts to offer. Move on and concentrate on how you can improve yourself to grow and succeed.

Remember, you and only you
are really in charge of you.

ALDOUS HUXLEY
ENGLISH NOVELIST AND ESSAYIST

"Experience is not what happens to a man. It is what a man does with what happens to him".

In other words, experience is not what happens in your life but the way you deal with the situation. An experience can be good, bad or indifferent but the result and how you deal with it is up to you.

In fact experience can either be a rear view mirror of what you have done in the past or a springboard to the future.

RALPH WALDO EVERSON
AMERICAN ESSAYIST, POET AND PHILOSOPHER

"What lies behind us and what lies before us are tiny matters compared to what lies within us".

This statement highlights the ability and power that lies within you, however this is latent until you tap your talent and put it to good use.

So open the door to new opportunities and challenges and find out just how talented you are.

Remember, you'll never ever know unless you give yourself the satisfaction of unlocking the treasure chest of ability that lies within you.

HENRY MILLER
AMERICAN AUTHOR

"Life is constantly providing us with new funds, new resources, even when we are reduced to immobility. In life's ledger there is no such thing as frozen assets."

This message is especially powerful in that it highlights that you are always able to think and grow rich in many ways even if you are experiencing a period of depression.

So don't give up and throw your hands in the air. Focus instead on the talents, friends and resources you have got and make them work for you.

ROBERT LOUIS STEVENSON
SCOTTISH NOVELIST, POET AND ESSAYIST

**"The world is so full of a number of things,
I'm sure we should all be as happy as kings."**

This quote reminds us that there is abundance in the world if we would only go and look for it. It is easy when you are down and depressed to only focus on the problem at hand.

Instead you must lift your eyes to the horizon, take in the world around you and remind yourself of the many beautiful things there are in life.

HENRY MILLER
AMERICAN AUTHOR

"Develop interest in life as you see it; in people, things, literature, music – the world is so rich, simply throbbing with rich treasures, beautiful souls and interesting people. Forget yourself."

This reinforces the fact that it is all too easy to simply focus on yourself in life. Instead realise that the world is full of rich, exciting and beautiful treasures and people.

So get out of your own space and explore the planet, the wildlife, the flowers and the people. You'll love it.

REINHOLD NIEBUHR
AMERICAN THEOLOGIAN
(NOW THE PRAYER OF ALCOHOLICS ANONYMOUS)

"God grant me the serenity to accept the things I cannot change, the courage to change the things I can and the wisdom to distinguish the one from the other."

This quote is momentous in itself and has given hope to many millions of people. My own brother who fought with the Australian troops in the Vietnam War lives by this philosophy and another A A quote which is very apt for us all, "Yesterday's history, tomorrow's a mystery".

JAMES RUSSELL LOWELL
AMERICAN POET AND ESSAYIST

"There is no good in arguing with the inevitable. The only argument available with an east wind is to put on your overcoat."

This simply reinforces the point that all too often in life your emotion can get the better of your objective judgement and take you in a direction that is wasteful.

Your pride often is to blame, when you should or could simply admit that you can't beat the situation and therefore focus on a more productive set of actions.

EDWARD EVERETT HALE
AMERICAN MINISTER AND WRITER

**"If you have accomplished
all that you have planned for yourself,
you have not planned enough."**

This message is very insightful
and I once experienced this myself.

It is evidence that many people do not set their
sights high enough and therefore set goals too low.

When these goals are achieved often you will easily
become bored and depressed, for you will not have set
yourself goals and tasks to stimulate your mind and
keep yourself not only busy but excited about life.

ANATOLE FRANCE
FRENCH WRITER

"To accomplish great things we must not only act, but also dream; not only plan, but also believe."

The quote highlights the power of dreaming and visualising what you want to achieve in life. It sets you on a path to greatness and gives you a focus and commitment to pursue your goals with a belief that you are on a road to your destiny.

Self belief is then the keystone in the archway of achievement and the attribute that will enable you to overcome any obstacles along the way.

FRIEDRICH VON SCHILLER
GERMAN HISTORIAN AND POET

"He that is over cautious will accomplish little."

How true this is in sport. When you are too careful all to often you lose the gifts god has given you to perform with flair and confidence.

It has been observed of many sporting teams and sports people. They initially think creatively and confidently believing in their ability. Then when leading they become too cautious and play negatively to protect their lead and give up the confident advantage they had over their competition, and all too often lose.

ROBERT F KENNEDY
PAST AMERICAN SENATOR AND ATTORNEY GENERAL

**"Only those who dare to fail greatly
can ever achieve greatly."**

This thought reminds me of a comment once made
by the then world's richest man, John Paul Getty,
the American oilman. His point was that to achieve
success in business and life you needed the one
ingredient that unsuccessful people don't possess,
the ability to take a calculated risk.

Captains of ships and planes especially are forever
taking calculated risks in the interests of the safety
of their passengers.

Try it, it gives you a feeling of great satisfaction.

LUC DE CLAPIERS
MARQUIS DE VAUVENARGUES, FRENCH NOVELIST AND WRITER

"To achieve great things we must live as though we were never going to die."

Yes, I agree. In 1974 I experienced this unique feeling. I started my own business with $500 and no clients. It was like looking over a cliff and seeing there was nowhere to land but believing there was!

All my friends and family told me I was mad and that I would surely fail. Well 35 years later I can tell you I succeeded. I took the leap of faith and landed safely.

JOHN F KENNEDY
FORMER PRESIDENT OF THE UNITED STATES OF AMERICA

"There are risks and costs to a programme of action but they are far less than the long range risks and costs of comfortable inaction."

Action and leadership are usually thought to apply to business, sport or war. Leadership, I believe, is also about you bringing up a family by being a role model, making rules, showing love and affection, enforcing discipline and giving advice and encouragement.

There are of course risks associated with this role, but they are far less than abdicating your responsibility.

GENERAL GEORGE PATTON
AMERICAN ARMY GENERAL

"A good plan violently executed right now is far better than a perfect plan executed next week."

This comment highlights the importance of taking action in your life and not sitting on the fence procrastinating. Too often you can be guilty of waiting for all the information necessary to make a decision and in the process lose the window of opportunity.

So when you have say 80 percent of the information required take a risk, make a decision and take action to implement your the plan. Usually you'll be glad you did.

CHARLES DE GAULLE
FRENCH PRESIDENT AND STATESMAN

"Deliberation is the work of many men. Action, of one alone."

How true this is today in life, business and sport.

Today teams are the key to success but the strategy, vision and goals must be created and owned by the team.
As a team member you must be empowered by your leader, captain or coach to believe in the plan and implement it with excellence.

However, you as the leader must take responsibility for putting the plan, vision or strategy into action and be accountable for the team in achieving the goals.

RALPH WALDO EMERSON
AMERICAN ESSAYIST, POET AND PHILOSOPHER

"Do the thing and you will have the power."

Waiting forever, sitting on your hands, scared to make the move, pondering what might go wrong. Is this you? Well if you want to gain power in your life and develop the self confidence that goes with it, then take action and do what you must do.

This action can also give you a special freedom to know that you have taken a positive approach to life.

Remember if you want power in your life, then have a focus for action.

WILLIAM SHAKESPEARE
ENGLISH PLAYWRIGHT AND POET

"Suit the action to the word, the word to the action; with this special observance, that you o'erstep not the modesty of nature."

Great words from a great person.

In other words, live your life with integrity and be who you say you are and do what you say you will do.

It is vital in life that you understand that your integrity is on show everyday for all to see.

So make sure you realise that the respect and trust you crave will only come from performing each day with total integrity and delivering the promise of expectation.

THEODORE ROOSEVELT
LONGEST SERVING PRESIDENT OF THE UNITED STATES

"Do what you can with what you have, where you are."

Too often we think and act through "rose coloured glasses" and see that the grass seems to be greener elsewhere.

How often is it though that when you seek the green grass, you find that it is really only a "mirage in your mind".

In business, for instance do you know it costs five times more to get a new customer than it does to keep an existing one.

LUC DE CLAPIERS, MARQUIS DE VAUVENARGUES
FRENCH NOVELIST AND WRITER

"Action makes more fortunes than caution" -
or as I have often heard in life,
"He that hesitates is lost."

How often have you heard that said in relation to a purchase, a decision or an opportunity?

Too often you can second guess yourself and worry what if, instead of getting off the fence you're sitting on and taking positive action.

Usually your judgement will be correct and the outcome successful. To sit on the fence of procrastination can often stop you taking the advantage.

F SCOTT FITZGERALD
AMERICAN NOVELIST

"Never confuse activity with action."

It's easy to satisfy your consciousness and your guilt by making yourself seem busy but not really doing anything worthwhile.

In life and business it's called Parkinson's Law. It's when you give a task to someone and they make the task fit the time.

To deter people from falling into this trap, it's important that you give yourself and them specific deadlines for tasks to be completed. When you do this you can plan better and achieve more and the other person will also feel more satisfied and proud.

CHARLOTTE BRONTÉ
ENGLISH NOVELIST

"It is vain to say human beings might be satisfied with tranquillity; they must have action and they will make it if they cannot find it."

If you are thinking about retiring, it is well-known that you can easily become bored and depressed if you retire without an activity plan in place.

Even if you have one, it is easy to become lost and lonely and a pain to your partner.

Remember, you will be happier and live longer too if you keep your brain active.

JOHN MILTON
ENGLISH POET

"Boast not of what thou wouldst have done, but do what then thou wouldst."

In other words, its easy and perhaps a cop out to feel proud of what you might have done and crave false adulation. However, it often takes more grit, determination and courage to actually take charge of yourself and do what is necessary at the time in a situation.

You should also feel more satisfied and proud because you are more genuine and authentic in your comments or story when you tell others of your exploits or achievements.

THOMAS FULLER
ENGLISH DIVINE AND HISTORIAN

"The great end of life is not knowledge but action."

What are you going to be remembered for achieving? It's a question I asked a client recently.

He had never considered the question before and found it surprisingly challenging to answer.

Well, what are you going to be remembered for?

Think about it, what have you achieved or what can you still achieve in your life. So don't just read, think or learn, get busy and do something significant you have always wanted to do.

BENJAMIN DISRAELI
ENGLISH STATESMAN AND WRITER

"There is no education like adversity."

At the time you don't realise it, but experiencing adversity is often the best way to learn.

Relationships, business ventures and projects that fail can often teach you powerful lessons of life.

In fact adverse experiences can often change your views and even your direction of life.

Remember, you wouldn't know what up was unless you had been down, what profit was unless you had experienced a loss, what health was unless you had been ill or what success was unless you had failed.

BEN JONSON
ENGLISH DRAMATIST

"He knows not his own strength that hath not met adversity."

It is often said that grown men shouldn't cry, but you will not allow yourself to grieve unless you do.

Once you have expressed your feelings you are able to rebuild and put down the foundations of your future.

Strength comes from finding the ability to cope with adversity. Handling adversity enables you to find out what you are really made of and enables you to learn to understand your strengths and weaknesses so you can grow in the future.

FRIEDRICH WILHELM NIETZCHE
GERMAN PHILOSOPHER AND CRITIC

"What does not destroy me makes me strong."

Often you despise people or events for what they do to you, but at the time you don't realise that in fact you are growing in strength.

When you experience these lessons in life you will often receive many subtle benefits and grow in statue and wisdom, but these lessons won't be easy.

Mental strength is what champions are made of and modern day sporting champions like Roger Federer, Tiger Woods, Usain Bolt or Ricky Ponting thrive on mental toughness.

SAMUEL JOHNSON
ENGLISH LEXICOGRAPHER, CRITIC AND WRITER

"Adversity is the state in which man most easily becomes acquainted with himself, being especially free of admirers then."

As they say you know who your true friends are when you experience adversity. How often are you shocked by people who seem good friends, not really caring and abandoning you when you are suffering in a time of need.

It can be a cruel experience, but at least it serves to show you how transparently false they really are as a so called friend. It can be a blessing in disguise.

DOLLY PARTON
AMERICAN COUNTRY AND WESTERN SINGER AND SONGWRITER

"The way I see it, if you want the rainbow, you gotta put up with the rain."

Many of you would surely agree and in fact, be pleased if it would only rain more often.

It's easy to want to win, reap the reward or be successful without experiencing the hard work required to make it happen.

As I often say achieving mediocrity is easy but achieving excellence is difficult. You have to show discipline and put in the extra effort in order to excel in life.

JOSH BILLINGS
AMERICAN HUMORIST

"Adversity has the same effect on a man that severe training has on a pugilist – it reduces him to his fighting weight."

When you experience adversity its like a fitness program for your mind. It can sharpen and strengthen your resolve to survive and succeed.

My advice however, is to focus on success and not survival as it makes you set your sights higher and raises your expectations.

As Edward de Bono states, "If you shoot to succeed you will survive but if you shoot to survive you will fail".

JONATHON SWIFT
ENGLISH ARTIST

"Every man desires to live long, but no man would be old."

Every man I know shudders at the thought of getting old, but perhaps the reason is because of your perception of what is old.

Old implies "not able to do anymore" to many men. It also implies a loss of strength, vision, vitality, speed, health and looks.

However, it doesn't imply a loss of intelligence, insight, charm, experience, knowledge or wisdom. You just need to realise that as you get older your strength comes from above the shoulders.

PLATO
GREEK PHILOSOPHER

"He who is of a calm and happy nature will hardly feel the pressure of age."

If you can be relaxed about your age and also have a laugh at yourself, then you can even become better with age.

Using self talk each day can also help you handle the pressure of age. Being a member of a club or group can also help keep age in perspective.

So when you don't play as well as you hoped next time at golf, tennis or bowls, remember at least your'e above the grass!

HENRY DAVID THOREAU
AMERICAN ESSAYIST, POET AND MYSTIC

"None are so old as those who have outlived enthusiasm."

Be yourself, believe in yourself and you will succeed in filling up your tank of enthusiasm.

Remember, young people like being around fun loving, witty, energetic older people. They say enthusiasm is contagious and has a magical power to encourage and lift people's spirits.
Have you tried it lately?

It can give your friends a super shot of inspiration and change the whole atmosphere of a meeting and make people feel glad to be alive.

BRIGITTE BARDOT
SEXY FRENCH ACTRESS

"It's sad to grow old, but nice to ripen."

Many people you meet are actually doing this daily.

Age can be like a product life cycle, it can tell you how old you are but not what condition you are in. That is up to you!

Many people are handicapped by immaturity in their earlier years, but become more valuable to society as they mature and ripen. As you've heard people say, she's just like a good wine, she's maturing with age!

What a lovely compliment.

T.S. ELIOT
AMERICAN BORN POET AND DRAMATIST

"The years between fifty and seventy are the hardest. You are always being asked to do things, and you are not yet decrepit enough to turn them down."

Yes, but how wonderful it is.

Young people really want the help, advice and wisdom of a mature person when they are still maturing. What a compliment it can be to be asked to help others in these twilight years.

It is often said that the best years for a prime minister to be in office are the years between fifty and seventy.

DOROTHY CANFIELD FISHER
AMERICAN NOVELIST

"One of the many things nobody ever tells you about middle age is that it's such a nice change from being young."

How often have you heard a friend say, "I wish I was her age and know what I know now!"

Be grateful in the fact that middle age brings with it serenity and also enables you to develop and achieve your full potential in life.

Being young is great, but growing older is even greater just as long as you stay young at heart!

MAURICE CHEVALIER
FRENCH SINGER AND ACTOR

"I prefer old age to the alternative."

In today's changing world people are resisting change and it's a fact that the older we are the more habitual we become and the more we resist change. We can't say any more "what goes up must come down" – because satellites stay up!

Change is everywhere at present, in fact it's interesting to know that it's impossible to currently draw a graph of change for many industries.

The telecommunications industry for instance, is changing as I speak.

JOSEPH CAMPBELL
THE IRISH POET

"As a white candle in a holy place, so is the beauty of an old face."

I remember my mother in her twilight years and the beauty of her old face. She went blind and couldn't walk, but her brain was like a desk top computer!

At age 92 she passed away, but only a year before she gave an address to the local mayor, councillors, management and staff, on behalf of the residents, to celebrate the opening of a new facility.

Her face lit up and she didn't miss a beat!

BERNARD BARUCH
AMERICAN FINANCIER AND PRESIDENTIAL ADVISER

"I will never be an old man. To me, old age is always 15 years older than I am."

The power of the mind is amazing. Telling yourself in self talk that you are young is a beginning.

Thinking you are young and mixing with positive thinking people is an experience.

Acting like you are young and believing in yourself is exhilarating.

You are what you think of most of the time, so think young and cherish your time. Remember, the last 30 seconds are gone forever!

DANIEL-FRANCOIS-ESPRIT AUBER
FRENCH COMPOSER

"Ageing seems to be the only available way to live a long life.'

It seems a comment from a monty python show, but often stating the obvious reinforces a poignant point. When you think about it, at present there is no alternative, so why do we worry about ageing.

Is it our ego or pride or is it that we have a fantasy in our minds of always staying young.

I play golf with a friend Michael, who thinks he's Peter Pan and he is a joy to know.

GEORGE SAND (AMANDINE AURORE LUCIE DUPIN)
FRENCH NOVELIST

"One wastes so much time, one is so prodigal of life, at twenty! Our days of winter count for double. That is the compensation of the old."

It is often said that when you were twenty you thought you were bullet proof, could virtually walk on water and would live forever. You partied forever and lazed around and couldn't wait until you were 21.

However, once past that magical age the years start to flash by like a train as it speeds through the country side.

GOLDA MEIR
ISRAELI PRIME MINISTER

"Old age is like a plane flying through a storm. Once you're aboard there's nothing you can do. You can't stop the plane, you can't stop the storm, you can't stop time. So one might as well accept it calmly and wisely."

In other words, accept old age gracefully and rejoice in the fact that you are a child of nature and part of the universe.

Acceptance of one's life, for better for poorer, in sickness and in health is really the only way to love yourself unconditionally.

LEE TREVINO
AMERICAN GOLFER

"Grey hair is great, ask anyone who's bald".

Today, grey power has its place in life and even the business world is seeing a surprising resurgence of the older, experienced employee, consultant or coach.

Men, known in the past in commercial terms often as "the silver fox" are now in more demand to coach and mentor the young, ambitious executives.

It seems that the sporting benefits of coaching has at last been embraced by the business world as a way of accelerating the stars in their career.

JONATHAN SWIFT
ENGLISH SATIRIST

"No wise man ever wished to be younger."

Experience really is the foundation of the building of knowledge and wisdom. However, the getting of wisdom is only achieved by the gaining of knowledge and experience.

This seems a bit of a riddle but never the less is true of becoming wise.

Gaining confidence is also an interesting achievement in life, but can only really be gained when you know what you're doing and how to do it well. Effective public speaking is a great example of becoming wise in life.

FRED ASTAIRE
AMERICAN DANCER, SINGER AND ACTOR

"Old age is like everything else. To make a success of it, you've got to start young."

Fred started young and if you remember blossomed into singing and serious acting in his later life.

I also remember attending church as a boy with the well-known actor Lewis Fiander. He was young then too. Confident, flamboyant, arty, extroverted and a talented dancer.

He was educated in Melbourne, but travelled overseas to London where he developed his career on the stages of Europe before returning to Australia as a successful actor.

GLENDA JACKSON
ENGLISH ACTOR AND POLITICIAN

"I look forward to growing old and wise and audacious".

I think that encapsulates her very character and spirit she showed during her acting career.

How do you feel growing old? Are you feeling wise and audacious? Well, I am sure you feel you are a wiser person now than when you were younger, but do you feel audacious?

I meet a lot of people who I feel are audacious who are also OK with themselves as they become older. They just seem to take themselves less seriously and in fact develop a lovely self-depreciating sense of humour.

DAME MARY GILMORE
AUSTRALIAN POET

"Youth troubles over eternity, age grasps at a day and is satisfied to have even the day."

Our youth at university have been an example over the years of worrying about what might become, even before they have qualified with their degree.

Today our youth seem to still be troubled over the future when they are not aware of all the facts.

However, you as an older person have the opportunity and wisdom to see a different perspective and often a more considered and informed view, and to really be the voice.

ALEXANDER SMITH
SCOTTISH POET

"On the whole, I take it that middle age is a happier period than youth."

Well, it should be don't you think? You usually know where you're going, know who you are, know who your friends really are, and know what's going on in the world.

It seems that a middle aged person is more informed about world events and issues on average.

To prove this I have been researching what the United Nations stands for in the world and who runs it, and it seems many younger people don't really know.

HENRI FREDERIC AMIEL
SWISS POET AND PHILOSOPHER

"To know how to grow old is the master work of wisdom and one of the most difficult chapters in the great art of living."

How are you coping with your retirement?
Do you have a plan to keep your brain active and keep your body in shape?

Well, if you don't, chances are you will not cope or adjust well and will instead become older quicker.

In addition, the endorphins in your brain will turn off quicker and you will lose the ability to think young.

JOSEPH JOUBERT
FRENCH WRITER

"The evening of a well spent life brings its lamps with it."

In your older years you have the benefit of hind sight, which our younger people don't have yet, but how many of you have put this to good use in mentoring them?

Today our young people more than ever are looking for support, meaning and role models to help them form their lives and values.

Make sure you give of yourself freely, because often young people are shy and don't have the confidence to ask.

JOHANN WOLFGANG VON GOETHE
GERMAN POET, NOVELIST AND PLAYWRIGHT

"Everybody wants to be somebody; nobody wants to grow."

It is not easy today to understand that you have to study, learn, gain experience and perform in order to gain a position or even a promotion.

Young people, it seems from what I have observed, too often think that obtaining a degree automatically will enable them to be somebody in an organization when they graduate.

Well this isn't necessarily true, but having a degree will enable you to be employed quicker and if you perform well, promoted quicker.

ROBERT BROWNING
ENGLISH POET

"Ah, but a man's reach should exceed his grasp, or what's a heaven for?"

How high do you set your goals?
Do you even set goals?
It doesn't matter what age you are, humans perform more effectively if they set goals.

However, the goals should be reachable even though you need to stretch yourself to reach them.

So make your goals "smart goals".
S for specific   M for measurable   A for achievable
R for realistic and especially T for time sensitive
Then you will be more likely to achieve them.

HENRY WADSWORTH LONGFELLOW
AMERICAN POET

"If you would hit the mark, you must aim a little above it; every arrow that flies feels the attraction of earth."

How high do you shoot in life? do your eyes look up at your goals?

I often am told by clients that they don't set goals. Well, if you don't, there is no focus in your life and you will be rudderless and wander.

The key, however, is to set your goals so you have to stand on your toes to reach them.

WILLIAM BLAKE
ENGLISH POET, ARTIST AND MYSTIC

**"No bird soars too high
if he soars with his own wings."**

Often too many of us want to hold on to the coats or wings of others and get the easy ride.

However, those of you who do this I'm sure will admit, you don't have or get the same self satisfaction as if you had put in the hard work yourselves.

It's hard work though, to be passionate and disciplined enough to put in the effort to study, perform, act or research so you can soar with your own wings.

BENJAMIN ROBERT HAYDON
ENGLISH PAINTER

> **"When a man is no longer anxious to do better than well, he is done for."**

It's often called "losing the fire in your belly" or the passion to perform at the highest levels.

You see it in sports such as golf and tennis, in businesses run by self-made people and in life, when people give up or retire and set no goals to achieve.

If you are in any of these categories, I suggest you see or obtain a DVD of the wonderful film *The Bucket List*.

THOMAS HENRY HUXLEY
ENGLISH BIOLOGIST

"The rung of a ladder was never meant to rest upon, but only to hold a man's foot long enough to enable him to put the other somewhat higher."

In other words, treat a ladder as a means or a metaphor for achieving higher things in life.

However, this is difficult for some people to execute or understand. Some time ago a friend of mine made the comment that he thought I was too ambitious and that I should remain who I was and be happy to be that person.

My answer to him was what person?

WILLIAM BLAKE
ENGLISH POET, ARTIST AND MYSTIC

"I was angry with my friend, I told my wrath, my wrath did end. I was angry with my foe; I told it not, my wrath did grow."

It's important for your quality of life to manage your anger but I know it's hard to achieve.

As humans, we defend our rightness and waste effort and energy.

Is it our pride that gets in the way of good sense and logic? If you have any worthwhile self-esteem and ego you will have pride. But be careful, pride is a double edged sword and can hurt you.

THOMAS DE QUINCEY
ENGLISH WRITER

"Man should forget his anger before he lies down to sleep."

I can remember my mother giving me advice before I got married that if I ever had a disagreement with my wife to always kiss and make up before we went to sleep.

How insightful she was.

It is an important key for newly weds and also for those who have been married for many years.

Or is it one of the secret ingredients in enabling a long marriage or relationship to blossom, survive and be successful?

JAMES PATRICK DONLEAVY
IRISH-AMERICAN WRITER

"When you don't have any money, the problem is food. When you have money, it's sex. When you have both, it's health. If everything is simply jake, then you're frightened of death."

It's commonly called anxiety syndrome. You're so anxious to be right, correct, pretty, beautiful, handsome, clever, suave and successful that you show it and cause yourself distress.

Instead, handle what you have and the cards you've been dealt and realise how lucky you are to be healthy and alive … and celebrate.

HENRY WARD BEECHER
AMERICAN CLERGYMAN

**"Clothes and manners do not make the man;
but when he is made,
they greatly improve his appearance."**

How often have we seen a man who looks
the part but lacks substance and integrity
when he performs or talks.

Are you conscious of this important fact in your
life? If so, you will know that it is the character and
values that make the person.

So if you look in the mirror and don't like what you
see, remember you have the power to change
"the you" in your life.

HELENA RUBENSTEIN
AMERICAN COSMETICS MANUFACTURER

"There are no ugly women, only lazy ones."

What a provocative statement,
but obviously true in her view.

My experience in life as a coach, father and husband, however, also confirms this to be true. I can remember my daughters growing up and trying to cope with their university commitments as well as work experience commitments.

Time was always an issue, but they always made the time to look their best. Pride also played an important part in planning and setting their values and high standards. Do you have pride in yourself?

WILLIAM HAZLITT
ENGLISH ESSAYIST

"Good temper is one of the greatest preservers of the features."

It's interesting to know that bad temper creates, not only distress or bad stress in your body, but worry lines on your face and as you may have observed a down turned mouth.

Good temper on the other hand creates "eustress" or good stress and helps you to laugh and be happy with your eyes shinning bright.

When you laugh and show happiness you also exercise all the muscles in your face, which help preserve your young looks.

SAMUEL JOHNSON
ENGLISH CRITIC AND WRITER

"Our aspirations are our possibilities."

Have you ever had a dream or a goal that you wanted to achieve at a young age?

Maggie Thatcher, the well-known English Prime Minister, had a goal or aspiration at age 13 to become the Prime Minister of England and she did.

My eldest daughter Nicole had a goal at age 13 to become a Solicitor and she did.

My goal at an early age was to have my own radio program and I have.

What do you aspire to become or do?

JOHANN WOLFGANG VON GOETHE
GERMAN POET

"We can always redeem the man who aspires and tries."

In life, business and sport it is said it is always better to have tried and failed than to not have tried at all.

How often have you seen people give up and not try just when success was within their grasp?

But how do you expect to be forgiven or respected if you just give up without trying?

So if you want respect in life, remember to focus on the "umph" or effort and you will triumph!

NORMAN VINCENT PEALE
AMERICAN WRITER AND MINISTER

"Attitudes are more important than facts."

This is especially true when selling
or negotiating in a difficult environment.

Setting the climate for a serious discussion is
important in enabling both parties to build rapport
Watching your mood and manner at this stage of
the negotiation is vital in communicating your
attitude towards the discussion.

When presenting the facts, remember your attitude
can change how your information is accepted.
Research shows that 80 to 90 percent of all
communication is unspoken.
So remember your attitude sets your altitude.

OSCAR WILDE
FAMOUS IRISH POET, WIT AND DRAMATIST

**"We are all in the gutter
but some of us are looking at the stars."**

Why do many of you often see an issue
as the glass being half full whilst others see
the same issue as the glass being half empty?
Why does this happen to you?

Is it your value system handed down over
generations, your environment as you were
growing up or your experiences in life?

Do you know that it takes more energy and effort to
think that the glass is half empty than it does
to think it's half full? So make life less stressful
and think positively!

WILLIAM SHAKESPEARE
ENGLISH DRAMATIST AND POET

**"Nothing is good or bad,
but thinking makes it so."**

It is said that you are what you think of most of the time and therefore you are a by-product of your environment and your thinking.

Your brain is so powerful, but you can easily misuse it and create negative, bad, distressing thoughts, which can influence and lower your self esteem.

Your ability to control your thinking is therefore vital in having a high, positive self esteem.

Remember, it's OK to use daily self talk to tell yourself you're OK!

OG MANDINO
AMERICAN AUTHOR

"Take the attitude of a student. Never be too big to ask questions. Never know too much to learn something new."

I often find people are reluctant to ask questions at a coaching session or meeting. They often tell me they are worried they might make a fool of themselves.

Well if you do this and not ask questions you will make a fool of yourself anyway, because it's foolish to not ask questions.

As a mentor of mine once said, "You can always tell a paranoid but you can't tell them much".

WILLIAM JAMES
AMERICAN PSYCHOLOGIST AND PHILOSOPHER

"The greatest revolution of our generation is the discovery that human beings, by changing the inner attitudes of their minds, can change the outer aspects of their lives."

People often tell me their problems and how they are not able to think positively to solve them.

If you have the same problem, I suggest you change the message your brain has been programmed to receive, from negative to positive.

In psychological terms this is called self-talk and self-visualization. So take out the negative CD in your necktop computer and put in a positive one.

HENRY DAVID THOREAU
AMERICAN ESSAYIST, POET AND MYSTIC

"If a man does not keep pace with his companions, perhaps it is because he hears a different drummer. Let him step to the music which he hears, however measured or far away."

In life, we are not allowed to own, control or be responsible for our partner's work ethic, life, finances, habits, friends or values.

So don't hold your partner up, let them learn and fall down to their own beat. Just be loyal enough to care and help them up again so they can succeed.

ELISABETH KUBLER-ROSS
SWISS-BORN AMERICAN PSYCHIATRIST

"People are like stained-glass windows. They sparkle and shine when the sun is out, but when the darkness sets in, their true beauty is revealed only if there is a light from within."

Is your light burning bright after the sun sets? Are you doing things you enjoy with people you enjoy?

If not, set yourself a goal to turn on the light and seek like minded people with like minded interests.

However, you'll have to take a risk sometimes and put yourself in a new and different space to see the light.

JANE AUSTEN
ENGLISH NOVELIST

"To look almost pretty is an acquisition of higher delight to a girl who has been looking plain for the first fifteen years of her life than a beauty from her cradle can ever receive."

It's the focus of many songs of the past and "When I was 17" is just one of them!

Young girls aren't often blessed with what our demanding society calls good looks until they mature in later life.

So if you're a parent or grandparent, be patient and caring and you will see them turn into beautiful, graceful swans!

VITA SACKVILLE-WEST
ENGLISH WRITER, POET AND RENOWNED GARDNER

"It is very necessary to have makers of beauty left in a world seemingly bent on making the most evil ugliness."

It's interesting to compare a life coach or mentor with a terrorist! One sets about building another person's self-confidence, security, trust, success and self-esteem so the other person can succeed and win in life to achieve their full potential.

The other sets about destroying another person's self-confidence, security, trust, success and self-esteem so *they* can succeed and win in life to achieve *their* full potential.

JACQUELINE BISSET
ENGLISH ACTRESS

"Character contributes to beauty. It fortifies a woman as her youth fades. A mode of conduct, a standard of courage, discipline, fortitude and integrity can do a great deal to make a woman beautiful."

Other well-known actresses like Bridget Bardot, Jane Fonda, Judi Dench and Sophia Loren have all shown this exemplary mode of conduct and attributes as they have grown older.

They also have had the courage to pursue noble causes and lend their names and image to assist and raise awareness and funds.

RALPH WALDO EMERSON
AMERICAN ESSAYIST, POET AND PHILOSOPHER

"Though we travel the world over to find the beautiful, we must carry it with us or we find it not".

How often do we travel overseas to seek out the beauty of the world only to return and realise we have not yet seen the beauty of our own country?

People also seek out other friends and partners believing they will find another type of beauty only to find it is a mirage and does not really exist at all.

So each day see the beauty in your life.

JEAN ANOUILH
FRENCH DRAMATIST

"Things are beautiful if you love them."

Pat Boone once sang "love is a many splendid thing" he was right.

Partners, children, friends and colleagues are all beautiful if you love them, but the key to them knowing you love them is not to take them for granted.

Communication, therefore is the key to ensuring you convey your feelings of love. Many parents I fear only tell their children they love them when they are nearing the end of their life. What a waste of the opportunity and a tragedy of life.

RICHARD HENRY HORNE
ENGLISH WRITER

"'Tis always morning somewhere in the world."

Starting something special is exciting, but the hardest part is to actually start.

Setting an end date is an important part of the process. As Dr Steven Covey said in his book *The Seven habits of Highly Effective People*, "Begin with the end in mind".

Once you think through your plan and set your finish time, you will find it easier to start.
So when you want to achieve something special, remember you need a plan, discipline and a time commitment for action.

JOHANN WOLFGANG VON GOETHE
GERMAN POET, NOVELIST AND PLAYWRIGHT

"Whatever you can do or dream you can, begin it. Boldness has genius, power and magic in it."

Today people respond to and respect a leader with vision and a plan for achievement.

However, many business leaders I have met think that having a vision is a waste of time and effort.

Well, would you regularly get on a plane if you didn't know its destination?

Of course not, but leaders who don't have a vision are expecting their employees to board their plane and fly with them!

LAO-TZE
CHINESE PHILOSOPHER AND FOUNDER OF TAOISM

"A journey of a thousand miles must begin with a single step."

Many people have dreamt of starting their own business but either don't have the knowledge or the courage to take the first step.

Well, if you consider that your dream is the first step, then you can believe you already have the courage to proceed and succeed.

The next step is to talk to someone you can trust who has the knowledge to help you develop your plan.

Remember, just take the first step.

EUGENE F. WARE
AMERICAN LAWYER AND VERSE-WRITER

"All glory comes from daring to begin."

Whether you want to write a book, learn to paint, learn to play tennis, golf or bowls, you need to have the desire to begin.

If you want the acknowledgement, recognition and rewards then you must also have the courage to be bold and begin.

Take small steps to begin with so you can cope with the challenge. Then increase your stride as you gain skills and confidence.

Soon you will be enjoying your new found talent and feel the satisfaction of being fulfilled.

EILEEN CADDY
CO-FOUNDER OF THE FINDHORN FOUNDATION IN SCOTLAND

"The secret of making something work in your lives is first of all, the deep desire to make it work: then the faith and belief that it can work: then to hold that clear definite vision in your consciousness and see it working out step by step, without one thought of doubt or disbelief."

Self-belief is a strange,
but powerful attribute to have in life.

On one hand it can overflow and be offensive.
On the other hand it can inspire you
and others to deeds of greatness.

BENJAMIN NATHAN CARDOZO
AMERICAN JURIST

"We are what we believe we are."

The well-known American sports psychologist, Dr Dennis Whately, who was once appointed to assist the USA olympic track and field team as well as the NASA moon astronauts, also made the point in a slightly different way when he said, "We are what we think of most of the time".

What sort of person do you think you are? Do you believe you are someone special and a worthy person? If you don't, chances are you won't feel special and especially worthy.

FRANK LLOYD WRIGHT
AMERICAN ARCHITECT

"The thing always happens that you really believe in; and the belief in a thing makes it happen."

Visualization is often not understood, but sports people especially understand it. It is associated with self-belief, but you need in the first place to believe in yourself.

In Beijing, when China staged the Olympic Games on the 8th of the 8th month, 2008, athletes from around the world used this very powerful form of self-actualization.

Why don't you become an athlete of life and practise your own visualization and self-belief too?

WILLIAM JAMES
AMERICAN PSYCHOLOGIST AND PHILOSOPHER

"Believe that life is worth living, and your belief will help create the fact."

It's often called, "being on a roll", being up-beat, feeling confident, strutting your stuff, being fun to be around. In fact, just loving life to the full.

Successful business people tell me that it's their self-belief and positive attitude that makes the difference and helps them win.

Others tell me how bad it is, how tough it is and how gloomy it is.

As Rudyard Kipling once said, "You've got to think high to rise!

HENRY FORD
AMERICAN MOTOR CAR MANUFACTURER

"Whether you believe you can do a thing or believe you can't, you are right."

In other words, it is your self-belief and your attitude that determines your ability and willingness to win.

How often have you nearly given up setting up a home entertainment component or a mobile phone? Then you sit and ponder what the problem might be and you tackle the task with new vigour and win.

I did recently. It was wonderful, but I had to believe I could first.

RALPH WALDO EMERSON
AMERICAN ESSAYIST, POET AND PHILOSOPHER

"Belief consists in accepting the affirmations of the soul; unbelief in denying them."

It's often called your sixth sense.
The female sex, I'm told, have it in spades. We males, I believe, have it but don't understand we do.

It's about believing in your inner instincts and acting on them.

How often have you had a feeling about something or someone and you have tried to brush it away, only to experience later that your judgement was right all the time.

FRIEDRICH WILHELM NIETZSCHE
GERMAN PHILOSOPHER AND CRITIC

"One does not know – cannot know – the best that is in one."

It's called by many people your full potential, your best, but how are you able to achieve your full potential?

Well, first you must believe in yourself enough to take a risk or two to give yourself the opportunity.

Second, you need to be able to work or play in an environment that enables you to display your skills and abilities.

Thirdly, you need to think, create and imagine and want to succeed badly enough to be your best.

W. SOMERSET MAUGHAM
ENGLISH WRITER

**"It is a funny thing about life;
if you refuse to accept anything but the best,
you very often get it."**

It's a powerful quote, but one which can work for you in life, business and sport.

It 's often associated with a phenomenon called a self-fulfilling prophecy. Being assertive and demanding in life of having the best you can have is also often associated with the strength of your mind.

It's all about setting your goals, standards and values and believing not only you'll get them, but believing also you're worth having them.

SIR WINSTON CHURCHILL
ENGLISH STATESMAN

"I am easily satisfied with the very best."

Are you easily satisfied with the very best,
or easily satisfied with nearly the very best?

It's a valuable lesson I learned about how a nursing home handled and cared for their residents.

The management were pre-occupied in saving money and making a profit, instead of striving for the very best and making sure it was always delivered to people who not only had earnt it, but deserved it.

The words they often used to satisfy residents were – probably, usually, normally, but never always!

THOMAS A. EDISON
AMERICAN INVENTOR

"There is a better way to do it; find it."

Are you satisfied with mediocrity in your life,
or do you wish you performed with excellence?

The famous figures of world history were never
satisfied with mediocrity and instead found a way
of finding and performing at their best, consistently.

You see, people in life who do famous things, think,
plan and do things that unsuccessful people don't
do in order to achieve their goals.

In the end, they become all that they
ever dreamed of becoming.

HENRY FORD
AMERICAN MOTOR CAR MANUFACTURER

"Believe in the best, think your best, study your best, have a goal for your best, never be satisfied with less than your best, try your best, and in the long run things will turn out for the best."

Perhaps it's about giving yourself a lifetime flight plan to soar high and achieve your best.

If you want a life you can look back on and be proud of, then you need a set of values, standards and goals that enable you to give of your best.

MAX BEERBOHM
ENGLISH WRITER AND CARICATURIST

"Only mediocrity is always at its best."

As I often say, it's easy to be mediocre, but it's difficult to be excellent in life, business and sport.

In fact, it's not just difficult, it's very tough to excel at what you do. You have to not only set goals, but you must be very disciplined and an exceptional time manager.

Generally speaking, those people who are the best organized are the best at achieving their best in life.

Do you manage your time,
or does your time manage you?

GUSTAVUS F. SWIFT
AMERICAN MEAT INDUSTRY MAGNATE

"Don't let the best you have done so far be the standard for the rest of your life."

Have you reached a stage in your life when you feel you have accomplished all you can?

This is a difficult time and it is usually a good time to see a coach or friend and explore opportunities to set some new goals and a new direction.

A friend once gave me some great advice – she said, "Don't turn right and lose it all, just veer right and use it all – for other people".

DAVID LLOYD GEORGE
BRITISH PRIME MINISTER

"Do not be afraid to take a big step if one is required. You can't cross a chasm in two small jumps."

It's correct, but you need great courage to achieve your destiny.

It is said, "It's safe to stay in your nest, but you never get to fly".

Mother birds are a great example of helping their young to have courage to grow and develop. When they have developed physically, she encourages them and often pushes them out of their nest. In doing so, they either die or fly!

ELIZABETH GOUDGE
ENGLISH AUTHOR

"Her birthdays were always important to her, for being a born lover of life, she would always keep the day of her entrance into it as a very great festival indeed."

Do you celebrate your birthdays with style and impact, or do you try to forget them and let them pass quietly by?

Birthdays are really a day to celebrate your arrival into the world and to be proud of yourself and who you have made as friends. They say we're here only a short time, not a long time, so if you are on the train of life and the world is rushing by, pull the cord and celebrate at a stop or two.

LORD BYRON
ENGLISH POET

"'Tis being and doing and having that make all the pleasures and pains of which mankind partake; to be what God pleases, to do a man's best, and to have a good heart, is the way to be blest."

Helping others, as a life policy, is a special way of giving and feeling you have made a difference.

But don't wait to be asked, seek out people who need your help.

The very thought of helping and of making someone else happy is a great way to feel you are lucky to be alive.

ROBERT LOUIS STEVENSON
SCOTTISH NOVELIST, POET AND ESSAYIST

**Go, little book, and wish to all
flowers in the garden, meat in the hall,
a bin of wine, a spice of wit,
a house with lawns enclosing it,
a living river by the door,
a nightingale in the sycamore.**

Have you found nature lately?

Why not venture out and take in some scenery and fresh air. It can be inspiring and invigorating!

Walk around a lake with friends or your iPod. Go to the gardens and take in the beauty.
Walk your dog. Just do it!

ALEXANDER POPE
ENGLISH POET

"Blest, who can unconcern'dly find
hours, days, and years, slide soft away
in health of body, peace of mind,
quiet by day,
sound sleep by night; study and ease
together mix'd; sweet recreation, and
innocence,
which most does please
with meditation.
Thus let me live, unseen unknown;
thus unlamented let me die;
steal from the world, and not a stone
tell where I lie."

I find the most powerful thought today in this busy, hectic, workaholic world is to create a life of balance.

Is your life in harmony and balance?

BUDDHA
THE FOUNDER OF BUDDHISM

"Now may every living thing, young or old, weak or strong, living near or far, known or unknown, living or departed or yet unborn, may every living thing be full of bliss."

In life today, we need bliss or perhaps many other words that mean this, such as peace.

In today's pressurised environment, the state of calmness seems to have almost vanished.

What are you doing to create your peace and tranquility?

So stop, take stock, smell the roses and create your peace.

HENRY DAVID THOREAU
AMERICAN ESSAYIST, POET AND MYSTIC

"How many a man has dated a new era in his life from the reading of a book?"

Have you read a good book lately or,
like many people, are you just too busy?

Going on a holiday is a great time to read. Whether on a plane, boat, ship or train, or just lazing by the pool, you can create time and space to read.

Often, a book will change your direction
in life and set you on a new journey with
new goals and dreams.

SAMUEL BEN JUDAH IBN TIBBON
FRENCH-JEWISH TRANSLATOR AND PHYSICIAN

> "Make books your companions, let your bookshelves be your gardens: bask in their beauty, gather their fruit, pluck their roses, take their spices and myrrh."

The stories of life and people's achievements I find fascinating.

Fiction is always a great escape from the real world you live in and can be breath-taking in its creativity.

Children, if encouraged, can learn to grow and develop by reading throughout their formative years. Have you grown your own book shelf garden yet so they can visit it?

MARTIN FARQUHAR TUPPER
ENGLISH WRITER

"A good book is the best of friends, the same today and forever."

Have you ever kept a special book you have read and enjoyed next to your bed so you can easily pick it up and read it again and again?

Some books, I know, don't lend themselves to this, but others do.

It's a good way to reinforce the stories and ideas you read. It's also a great way to help you relax and get to sleep easily, so you have a good night's rest.

HORACE GREELEY
AMERICAN JOURNALIST

"It is impossible to mentally or socially enslave a Bible-reading people. The principles of the Bible are the groundwork of human freedom."

Evidence of this was the release of Nelson Mandela, after 27 years in jail for trying to topple South Africa's apartheid regime.

Nelson Mandela recently celebrated his 90th birthday at a magnificent concert held in his honour where precisely 46,664 tickets went on sale, representing his prison number. Possibly the greatest man of our generation has now passed on the baton of the fight for freedom to new hands.

CHARLES DICKENS
ENGLISH NOVELIST

"The new testament is the very best book that was ever or ever will be known in the world."

When all other books have been read, the new testament will be the book that remains the benchmark of all books. It is a book which sets most of the rules for the world's morals and role models.

Unfortunately, we probably don't read it enough, later in life, but when times are hard and you need to be tough, it is the one book that you can rely on for help.

THOMAS CARLYLE
SCOTTISH ESSAYIST, HISTORIAN AND PHILOSOPHER

> **"All that mankind has done, thought, or been is lying in magic preservation in the pages of books."**

Yes, that is true; books are often the record of either a person's life, beliefs or experiences. You open your right brain and visualise when you read. It's a great way to learn and develop.

It's easy, though, to sit and let the TV screen do the work for you, but if this is all you do, you will be robbed of a special world of magic and mystery.

CHARLES W. ELIOT
ENGLISH EDUCATOR

"Books are the quietest and most constant of friends; they are the most accessible and wisest of counsellors, and the most patient of teachers."

In today's busy, stressful world, books can be a real help to guide you through your times of need.

They also enable you to create a quiet space for yourself and even perhaps a knowledge sanctuary.

You can take yourself away in your mind and quietly go on a journey of learning and discovery. Reading is also a smart way to improve your knowledge and gain wisdom.

HELEN HAYES
LATE AMERICAN ACTRESS

"We rely upon the poets, the philosophers, and the playwrights to articulate what most of us can only feel, in joy or sorrow. They illuminate the thoughts for which we only grope; they give us the strength and balm we cannot find in ourselves. Whenever I feel my courage wavering, I rush to them. They give me the wisdom of acceptance, the will and resilience to push on."

Have you let these gifted people influence you and your life lately?

HELEN KELLER
DEAF AND BLIND AMERICAN LECTURER, WRITER AND SCHOLAR

"Literature is my utopia. Here I am not disenfranchised. No barrier of the sense shuts me out from the sweet, gracious discourses of my book friends. They talk to me without embarrassment or awkwardness."

Reading is one of the great wonders of the world. You are able to think and fantasize without anyone challenging you on your views.

Books allow you to open up your senses and experience new things in your life without the worry of feeling uncomfortable. What a way to experience freedom!

THOMAS A. EDISON
AMERICAN INVENTOR

"The chief purpose of the body is to carry the brain around."

Do you know it has been calculated that the capacity of the brain is equivalent to the Empire State building in New York filled with personal computers?

The problem with us as human beings is that in metaphorical terms, we only normally use about 20 floors of the building, or about 25 percent of our brain's capacity.

So, why don't you refocus your life on using your brain more and challenging yourself to grow?

WOODROW WILSON
PAST PRESIDENT OF THE UNITED STATES

"I not only use all the brains I have, but all I can borrow."

It's interesting to compare the workings of the British Westminster system of Government with that of the United States.

In the Westminster system, those elected are expected to be the ones with the brains, intelligence and experience to govern and run the country effectively. Whereas, in the United States system, often the best most intelligent and experienced leaders in private enterprise are co-opted or appointed to ministerial positions to govern and run the country.

FRANKLIN P. JONES
AMERICAN CAPITALIST AND POLITICIAN

"Bravery is being the only one who knows you're afraid."

I was watching a telecast of an AFL football match recently when the well-known commentator described the actions of a player running backwards with the flight of the ball, as a pack of players were advancing, as a very brave action.

It made me think at the time, "I wonder how scared or afraid the player was in performing this feat".

Do you often wonder how afraid these courageous players are, when the put their bodies in danger?

SAMUEL JOHNSON
ENGLISH CRITIC AND WRITER

"It is worth a thousand pounds a year to have the habit of looking on the bright side of things."

Do you look on the bright side of life, or look on the dull side of life?

I have friends who do both, but the ones who see the bright side are the ones I enjoy being around.

It's a habit worth cultivating, because it's also less stressful and better for your health.

As the well-known Monty Python song says, "Always look on the bright side of life".

ARISTOTLE ONASSIS
GREEK SHIPPING MAGNATE

"The secret of business is to know something that nobody else knows."

It's called, 'having a point of difference' that can give you leverage.

When you know something, or do something that's special, you are able to put yourself or your business in a position of power and create what's called a "value proposition".

You see, people don't really buy price, they buy perceived value. So if your business is continually finding it difficult to survive, review your "value factor" or secret ingredient. As Peter Druker said, "Knowledge is power".

HENRY DAVID THOREAU
AMERICAN ESSAYIST, POET AND MYSTIC

"Beware of all enterprises that require new clothes."

How often have you been swayed into doing business with someone because of how well they are dressed?

It's become evident to me over the course of my life to date, that successful business people dress to match their market and not to impress their market.

I've also come to realize that most millionaires don't look like millionaires and that most people who look like they are millionaires, aren't. As the Japanese samurai warriors once said, "Deal with perception, not sight".

JAPANESE BUSINESS PHILOSOPHY

"Customer service is not a business slogan but a religion unto itself."

Some years ago, I asked the Professor of Marketing at the Tokyo University to compare how he saw the aspects of customer service in the USA, Australia and Japan.

He replied that the USA had sophisticated processes in place to react very quickly to customers' needs and that Australia was now realizing the importance of customer service and was starting to react to the problems and needs of customers. In Japan, he said, "We react before the customer tells us there is a problem".

JOSH BILLINGS
AMERICAN HUMORIST

"The happiest time in any man's life is when he is in red-hot pursuit of a dollar, with a reasonable prospect of overtaking it."

It's important for anyone, but it seems especially men, to be able to pursue a business dream in order to be happy and feel worthy.

This is very evident in marriage or relationship breakdowns, where the male is left by himself and his self-esteem and confidence are often very low.

Focusing himself on his business at that time is an excellent strategy to regain lost confidence, happiness and success.

HENRY FORD
AMERICAN MOTOR CAR MANUFACTURER

**"It is not the employer who pays wages –
he only handles the money.
It is the product that pays wages."**

Creating a product or service and producing it
to a consistently high level of quality excellence
is the secret of success today. Leadership, vision,
values and a caring culture are keys to enabling the
consistent delivery of the promise to the customer.

Today, more than ever however, it is having the
policies, procedures and processes in place and
your people knowing these, that ensures the
product pays the wages.

MICHAEL PHILLIPS
AMERICAN MOVIE PRODUCER

"Business should be fun. Without fun, people are left wearing emotional raincoats most of their working lives. Building fun into business is vital; it brings life into our daily being. Fun is a powerful motive for most of our activities and should be a direct path of our livelihood. We should not relegate it to something we buy after work with money we earn."

Is your business or job fun? If not, why not? As I often say, "You're at work more than you're home – it better be good!"

KATHARINE WHITEHORN
ENGLISH NEWSPAPER COLUMNIST

"The best careers advice to give to the young is find out what you like doing best and get someone to pay you for doing it."

It is often very difficult when you're young to really know what it is you would like to do for a career.

My suggestion is to make a list of all the things you like to do that make you the happiest.

It could also be a good idea to complete a SWOT analysis on yourself, listing your strengths, weaknesses, opportunities and threats.

JULIA MORGAN
AMERICAN ARCHITECT

"Never turn a job down because you think it's too small; you don't know where it could lead."

I remember once giving a talk to a small group of builders at the Housing Industry Association.

A member of the audience thought it was great and asked me to speak to his whole company, A V Jennings.

He eventually left and joined Jetset Travel, where he asked me to be guest speaker at their conference in Bangkok and train all Jetset's 1,250 retail staff and 400 head office personnel in Australia. Wow!

BENJAMIN FRANKLIN
AMERICAN STATESMAN AND PHILOSOPHER

"Plough deep while sluggards sleep."

In other words, putting in the hard yards and the extra effort can really pay off.

Building the foundations of your career is similar to laying the foundations of a high-rise building.

They take a long while to build; you usually don't see them and they are beneath the ground.

However, these foundations are the main reason that the building has the ability to rise to great heights. If you build your foundations early in your career, you too will rise to great heights.

HENRY DAVID THOREAU
AMERICAN ESSAYIST AND POET

"Things do not change: we change."

Change is a constant thing in life, but we are the ones who need to have the courage to change.

Unfortunately, as you get older it becomes harder to change as you get set in your ways and create habits.

I often tell my daughter Melinda, who is a doctor of psychology, a joke: "How many psychologists does it take to change a light globe?"

The answer is one – but the light globe has got to want to change!

HERACLITUS
ANCIENT GREEK PHILOSOPHER

"You can't step into the same river twice."

It's a subtle message for you to heed!

You see, the river is forever changing and you will find it impossible to experience the same exact feelings a second time.

It's like life, it's forever changing around us, but it still looks the same to our eyes.

The day of reckoning often comes when you see a friend again, that is about your age, after a long period of absence. It's then that you get the message that you've changed too!

MARCUS AURELIUS
ROMAN EMPEROR AND PHILOSOPHER

"We shrink from change; yet is there anything that can come into being without it? What does nature hold dearer, or more proper to herself? Could you have a hot bath unless the firewood underwent some change ... is it possible for any useful thing to be achieved without change? Do you not see, then, that change in yourself is of the same order, and no less necessary to nature?"

Today change is happening so fast that it is impossible to draw a graph of change before it's out of date!

HENRY BROOKS ADAMS
AMERICAN HISTORIAN, JOURNALIST AND TEACHER

"Chaos often breeds life, when order breeds habit."

Chaos it seems is a force that confuses. On one hand it can be stressful, disruptive and breed anxiety.

On the other hand it can breed change, excitement and anticipation into your life. At the time you probably don't see the benefits, but after the chaos has passed you will. Chaos is the cousin of change.

In business for instance it is said, "No change is stagnation, but uncontrolled change is chaos". So why not welcome a little chaos into your life.

FRIEDRICH WILHELM NIETZSCHE
GERMAN PHILOSOPHER AND CRITIC

"I say to you: one must have chaos in oneself in order to give birth to a dancing star."

Chaos can be likened in this case to feelings of uneasiness, un-acceptance or even unhappiness.

It's when you are feeling down, stressed, anxious or disillusioned that you often get an inspiration or a great idea.

This condition challenges you to think outside the square and it is then that you often will see a new way or a new solution to a problem.

Then like magic a star is born!

JAMES A. MICHENER
AMERICAN WRITER

"Character consists of what you do on the third and fourth tries."

As our parents used to say try, try, try again.

It is also said that many people give up just as they are about to be successful. It is a true test of character to keep on going in the face of all the odds and to keep focused on your goal.

As the American President Calvin Coolidge once said, "Persistence and determination alone are omnipotent or all powerful and show our true character to others."

JOHANN WOLFGANG VON GOETHE
GERMAN POET, NOVELIST AND PLAYWRIGHT

" Talent develops in quiet places, character in the full current of human life."

Many people hide away and work on their individual talent, keeping to themselves often like hermits. Artists have been renowned for this behavior for centuries.

However, you never get a chance to witness their character until they emerge in the brightness of day and display their works for all to see.

It is only then, when others can assess their efforts and vote with their mouths and money that they can show their true character.

HASIDIC SAYING

"In everyone there is something precious, found in no-one else; so honour each man for what is hidden within him – for what he alone has, and none of his fellows."

We are all special individuals with our own unique talents, but all too often we don't gain the recognition we deserve.

It also seems today that unless you conform to everyone else you are seen as out of step. This is often seen when a person takes a stand against an issue.

DAISY BATES
AUSTRALIAN SOCIAL WORKER

**"Surely the world we live in is
but the world that lives in us."**

It is said that you are a by product of your environment and that you are what you think you are most of the time.

Our mind is so powerful in shaping the world we live in, but we often mis-manage our mind and let it influence how and what we think of ourselves.

Remember, you and you alone have the ability to control how you feel and either be old at 40 or young at 80!

WILLIAM BLAKE
ENGLISH POET, ARTIST AND MYSTIC

"The tree which moves some to tears of joy is, in the eye of others, only a green thing which stands in the way. As a man is, so he sees."

We really have a powerful gift in each of us; we can either see the good in each other and make someone a special person or just see another ordinary body or person in our life.

It's easy to see the obvious attributes of someone, but it takes tolerance and insight to see the subtle talents and attributes of someone.

THOMAS JEFFERSON
PAST PRESIDENT OF THE UNITED STATES

"In matters of style, swim with the current; in matters of principle, stand like a rock."

In other words in life, mirror and match your friends and colleagues in style, presentation and speech, but when you believe you need to take a stand against a wrong, stand tall and strong and don't give in.

It's easy to take the easy way out but in matters of principle remember, if you don't stand for something you'll fall for anything.

THE TALMUD

"A man should endeavour to be as pliant as a reed, yet as hard as cedar wood."

Today this is more evident than ever. To be successful in life, sport but especially business, you need the ability to be both flexible and strong.

Flexible to bend with the circumstances, issues, opportunities and the environment, yet strong to perform consistently well under pressure and disciplined enough to follow the regulations and processes required for success.

It's a tough game to play, but one you need to play if you want to succeed and win.

ABRAHAM LINCOLN
PAST PRESIDENT OF THE UNITED STATES

"With malice toward none, with charity for all."

Were you brought up to believe that charity begins at home?

I was, but as my life unfolded I found the need to adjust and become more tolerant and forgiving.

Our values that are handed down now often need reflection and re-consideration to make them relevant.

For example, the fact that the world, through electronic communication, has become a global village, is a critical element that has possibly changed the world and our values forever.

ADRIENNE RICH
AMERICAN WRITER

> **"Only she who says she did not choose, is the loser in the end."**

Today you have the power to choose many things in life; your partner, your weight, your eating habits, your furniture, your friends, your vocation, your mobile phone, and even your attitude.

So when you get up each morning, pull up the blinds and look out the window, just realise you are in charge of you and put a positive CD in your neck top computer.

Remember, it's your attitude
that helps your success, so choose wisely.

HENRY ALFRED KISSINGER
GERMAN-AMERICAN STATESMAN AND UNIVERSITY PROFESSOR

"The absence of alternatives clears the mind marvellously."

How often have you been perplexed by having too much choice when buying a suit, a dress, a pair of shoes, a car, a kitchen setting or a meal?

Henry Ford perhaps had the right idea when he said you can have any Model T Ford you like, as long as it's black.

So if you want to clear your mind and stop procrastinating, limit the range of options you have to choose from and you'll make a wiser decision.

LADY CILENTO
DOCTOR, MEDICAL JOURNALIST AND NUTRITIONIST

"Only by keeping the past alive in our memories can we choose what to discard and what to retain in our present way of life."

We use memories as a reference framework to mould ourselves and shape ourselves as we grow.

For instance, when you have experienced grief you will often experience memories of certain occasions through songs, landmarks, or pictures that take you back in time.

These are called "souvenirs of the past" and when they happen you need to understand that they are normal and you're OK!

ROBERT FROST
AMERICAN POET

"Two roads diverged into a wood, and I – I took the one less travelled by, and that has made all the difference."

When you are confronted with a significant decision, it is a wise person who considers the options and takes the clearest, simplest one.

In life, business and sport we often over complicate our lives and put ourselves through unnecessary stress by making poor decisions.

As a rule, select the option that will give you the best result with the minimum amount of heartache. Your health will be better for it.

WILLIAM JAMES
AMERICAN PSYCHOLOGIST AND PHILOSOPHER

"When you have to make a choice and you don't make it, that itself is a choice."

It's often called a stand off or time out and it can be a very powerful form of assertion.

Often we can be pushed into making a choice and feel pressured by someone's actions, but it can be reassuring and gratifying sometimes to simply make a decision to not make a decision.

This action can be especially useful when you don't feel you have all the facts to make a wise decision.

CHARLES DARWIN
ENGLISH NATURALIST

"Whenever I have found that I have blundered or that my work has been imperfect, and when I have been contemptuously criticised and even when I have been overpraised, so that I have felt mortified, it has been my greatest comfort to say hundreds of times to myself that 'I have worked as hard and as well as I could, and no man can do more than this.'"

Have you ever felt guilty of beating yourself up unnecessarily over making a mistake when it's not entirely your fault?

Well don't!

ROBERT HERRICK
ENGLISH POET

**"And this for comfort thou must know:
Times that are ill won't still be so;
Clouds will not ever pour down rain;
A sullen day will clear again."**

It's hard, I know when everything around you is crumbling and you're feeling low, to think that the sun will shine again and you'll be okay.

You don't realise at the time that this situation is often a significant learning and growing experience.

The keys to coping through these times are to seek comfort with your friends and write down your plans for the future.

ANEURIN BEVAN
BRITISH LABOUR POLITICIAN

"We know what happens to people who stay in the middle of the road. They get run over."

Are you guilty of procrastination and not being committed in your actions and daily life?

Those who are, will often either be run over or passed in life by those who are committed.

It's easy though to take the easy way out and stay in the middle of the road.

The problem is however, if you don't make a decision you will never know what might have eventuated or how successful you might have been.

SIR WINSTON CHURCHILL
ENGLISH STATESMAN AND WARTIME PRIME MINISTER

"I have nothing to offer but blood, toil, tears and sweat."

There is something satisfying about getting involved in a good cause. I am not saying war was or is a good cause, but he had to get involved as England was under attack.

However, there are lots of peaceful good causes in the community, like Doxa, Camcare, the Red Cross and many others that you can get involved with and help.

The resulting commitment will give you a good feeling of satisfaction.

INDIRA GANDHI
INDIAN STATESMAN AND PRIME MINISTER

"You cannot shake hands with a clenched fist."

Today more than ever, you need to compromise on stressful, delicate, sensitive issues or situations. It's called a win-win outcome by Dr Stephen Covey in his book, *The Seven Habits of Highly Effective People*.

It's easy though to let emotion and the negative attitude of others influence you to become rigid and not give some ground in a negotiation, issue or situation.

The key for compromise is to use empathy and put yourself in the shoes of the other person.

MARY ANN EVANS
BETTER KNOWN AS GEORGE ELIOT, ENGLISH NOVELIST

"The beginning of compunction is the beginning of a new life."

Showing compunction or perhaps strength and tenacity as we know it, is a hallmark of people who make a success of their lives.

Having a conscience and wanting to do the right thing is a starting point for you to make a tough decision to take a proper course of action.

In business management it can make you more effective as a leader when you make the hard, but right, decision knowing the consequences of your actions and how it will effect others.

ANDREW CARNEGIE
SCOTTISH-AMERICAN INDUSTRIALIST AND PHILANTHROPIST

"Concentration is my motto. First honesty, then industry, then concentration."

Do you concentrate on achieving your goals? Do you know how to concentrate to achieve your goals?

It's not easy to master. You need firstly though to have set one or some attainable goals that you want to achieve. Then you need to set and write down some steps in order to achieve them.

Once you have done this, the key to achieving them is to block out any distractions and concentrate on the steps so you will be successful.

SAMUEL SMILES
SCOTTISH AUTHOR AND SOCIAL REFORMER

"The shortest way to do many things is to do only one thing at once."

Do you do too many things at once?
How often have you thought to yourself,
I wish I could achieve more?

Well one way to accomplish this goal is to focus on doing only one thing at once, but doing it well.

Your concentration level will increase
as well as your confidence.

As the world's greatest golfer Jack Nicklaus said,
"Do one thing well and the others will follow".

WALTER SAVAGE LANDOR
ENGLISH POET AND WRITER

"A man's vanity tells him what is honour; a man's conscience what is justice."

Does your conscience ever get the better of you? If it does chances are you're getting conscience confused with honour.

It's not easy sometimes to see or know the difference, but there is a difference. Pride is the cousin of vanity and can easily colour your judgement and decision making in the search to be honourable.

However, your conscience and the consequences of your actions are, in the long run, what enables you to achieve justice.

ROBERT GREEN INGERSOLL
AMERICAN AGNOSTIC

"In nature there are neither rewards nor punishments – there are consequences."

In other words in nature there are neither rights nor wrongs just results. In life this is often the same, but there are judgements associated with the issues – right judgements or wrong judgements. In business there are also judgements, but normally more decisions that have the effect of making consequences. I call this "consequential management". In other words you will be judged and assessed and suffer the consequences of your actions.

So consider the consequences before you act or make a significant decision.

ALPHONSE KARR
FRENCH WRITER

"The more things change, the more they stay the same."

In other words, change that has been made simply to make a change will not improve anything.

One example is the AFL football changing the rule allowing the ball to be kicked into play after a behind before the goal umpire has finished signalling the score.

This is done in basketball but they don't have goal umpires waving flags, instead scorers simply press a button to change the scoreboard. So far it has not improved the AFL game.

GUILLAUME APOLLINAIRE
FRENCH POET

"Come to the edge, he said. They said: we are afraid. Come to the edge, he said. They came. He pushed them, and they flew ..."

How did you bring up your children?

Did you smother them, control them, protect them, or did you encourage them to take a risk, seek new horizons, have courage and fly?

I once knew a mother who did everything for her three girls. She redirected their mail, opened their mail and even managed their bank accounts.

It's a shame, but they never got to fly!

BHAGWAN SHREE RAJNEESH
INDIAN SPIRITUAL CULT LEADER

"There is only one courage and that is the courage to let go of the past, not to collect it, not to accumulate it, not to cling to it. We all cling to the past, and because we cling to the past we become unavailable to the present."

Have you let go of the past yet?

It's hard to do I know, but the alternative is to be known as a hoarder and a collector of souvenirs of the past.

So have courage and focus your mind on the present.

MARK TWAIN
AMERICAN WRITER AND HUMORIST

"Courage is resistance to fear, mastery of fear, not absence of fear."

Fear grips us all no matter who we are in life.
It's just how much it grips us that is the issue.

It can make us freeze if things go bad in business,
sad if things go bad in relationships and negative
if things go against us in sport.

The key to overcoming fear is to put
it in perspective.

This is the hallmark of champions.
They have the courage to confront their fear.

SAMUEL JOHNSON
ENGLISH WRITER AND CRITIC

"Courage is reckoned the greatest of all virtues, because, unless a man has that virtue, he has no security for preserving any other."

What is the real security?

Is it doing the same thing over and over again or is it trying something new, different and exciting?

Courage is the essential ingredient in enabling employers, inventors, scientists and partners to plan and achieve great things in life.

So if you want some security in your life you need to develop your level of courage and make it your greatest virtue.

KATHARINE HEPBURN
AMERICAN ACTOR

"What the hell – you might be right, you might be wrong – but don't just avoid."

It's easy to sit on the fence and not make a mistake. However, you really can reap the rewards of success if you jump off and just have a go.

When I was contemplating leaving my employment with a large oil company and starting my own business, I can remember asking a mentor of mine for his view.

He said to me then, "If you don't have a go, you'll never ever know".

Thanks Eric!

ELEANOR ROOSEVELT
FIRST LADY OF THE UNITED STATES

"You gain strength, courage and confidence by every experience in which you really stop to look fear in the face ... you must do the thing you cannot do."

Every soldier who has ever gone to war must have had to look fear in the face.

I know my brother John had to when he fought in Vietnam. This strength, courage and confidence has helped him to cope with life.

So have courage to look fear in the face and do the thing that you think you can't do.

ARTHUR KOESTLER
HUNGARIAN-BORN WRITER

"If the creator had a purpose in equipping us with a neck, he surely meant us to stick it out."

Have you suggested something lately? It makes you feel great don't you think?

Many people are afraid to take a position on a specific issue for fear they will be laughed at.

Well, just remember, if you're that courageous, people actually respect a person for thinking differently to themselves.

You see deep down they wish it was them having the courage to ask the question or make the suggestion.

RALPH WALDO EMERSON
AMERICAN ESSAYIST, POET AND PHILOSOPHER

"What a new face courage puts on everything."

I have friends Jacky, Neville and Henry who have all had a form of cancer – breast cancer, leukemia and bone marrow cancer. They went through some tough times, I realise, but they put on the bravest of faces.

They never complained about their treatment and even attended functions.

In fact, many people didn't even know they were ill until they were told.

They all put on a brave face and fortunately were soon back doing what they loved most – working.

MIGUEL DE CERVANTES
SPANISH WRITER

"A stout heart breaks bad luck."

It is said in business you only want to do business with someone or a company who is confident and makes you comfortable they are doing well.

When a recession sets upon us this fact is even more important.

You see, people only want to be seen as making wise decisions and if you portray that you are not doing well then they don't feel comfortable doing business with you.

So in tough times have a stout heart and you'll do well.

JOHN DRYDEN
ENGLISH POET AND DRAMATIST

"Presence of mind and courage in distress, are more than brave armies to procure success."

How do you react when your world is falling around you? It's tough, I know about it!

Well, having control of yourself and your mind in times of distress can help you overcome adversity. Try using self talk every morning and night to help your strength of mind.

I say five words to myself when things are getting me down, "I'm happy, lucky, healthy, wealthy and free!" Try them and see if they work for you.

MARY ANN EVANS
BETTER KNOWN AS GEORGE ELIOT, ENGLISH NOVELIST

"Any coward can fight a battle when he's sure of winning, but give me the man who has pluck to fight when he's sure of losing."

Courage can be seen in many ways in life, but often the most powerful way is when someone fights against great odds.

People are moved by those who fight hard against the odds.

So if you're fighting against the odds, fight hard in the knowledge that not only will people admire you, but you'll have a better chance of winning too.

AMELIA EARHART
AMERICAN AVIATIOR

"Courage is the price that life exacts for granting peace."

As you know it takes courage to negotiate for peace in a troubled world.

It also takes courage to accept the terms of the peace negotiations as often someone or some country has to give ground to settle an issue. Are you courageous in negotiating peaceful settlements in your life? If so, well done, if not take a good look at your motives.

Chances are that you are trying to settle on a win-lose strategy instead of a win-win strategy.

ALEXANDER SOLZHENITSYN
RUSSIAN WRITER

"If one is forever cautious, can one remain a human being?"

Or, as my father used to say to me a long time ago, "He who hesitates loses".

One Saturday when he collected me from cricket he asked how I had played. I said I had battled cautiously at number seven for about an hour and a half and made 25 runs.

He looked at me and said, "Don't forget you win matches by making runs on the scoreboard".

It changed my attitude and I became an opening batsman!

RALPH WALDO EMERSON
AMERICAN ESSAYIST, POET AND PHILOSOPHER

"Good manners are made up of petty sacrifices."

Good manners today, are often seen as unimportant by many people when, in fact, they are a guide to a persons upbringing, values and character.

Examples like standing up for an elderly person on public transport or men waiting back for a woman to enter or leave an elevator seem to now be good manners of the past.

I once remember telling my 10 year old son to wait for his 14 year old sister to get in the elevator first. She replied, "Dad that's sexist". Now at 34 she's not so sure!

MAXWELL MALTZ
AMERICAN MOTIVATIONAL WRITER

"Emptiness is a symptom that you are not living creatively. You either have no goal that is important enough to you, or you are not using your talents and efforts in striving toward an important goal."

Do you feel empty in your daily life? If you do, then analyse why you feel this way?

Is it that you haven't set goals, that are significant enough, or is it that you're not focussing on the goal or goals sufficiently enough?

Chances are you are not using your talents effectively enough either.

ANNA FREUD
AUSTRIAN PSYCHOANALYST

"Creative minds have always been known to survive any kind of bad training."

As a corporate coach, I can honestly say that this is true. Creative minds seek out the answers they need and don't dwell on the techniques or methodology being used.

Creative people use their right brain and have the ability to think laterally to embrace a message or passage of knowledge. They also more easily think outside the nine dots or, as we know it, outside the square and are able to be more resilient than others.

CYNTHIA HEIMEL
AMERICAN FEMINIST WRITER

"When in doubt, make a fool of yourself. There is a microscopically thin line between being brilliantly creative and acting like the most gigantic idiot on earth. So what the hell, leap."

So when you are passionate about an idea, take a stand, and just say what you believe in.

Too often we worry about what others will think of us instead of just saying what we believe in.

Just remember, when you take the leap have faith in yourself and show respect to others.

ELBERT HUBBARD
AMERICAN WRITER

"To avoid criticism, do nothing, say nothing, be nothing."

Life is a test of your character and your upbringing. It is said, once a child turns seven, they are cast in stone forever.

As parents and grandparents, are you teaching your children and grandchildren the best you can, to be someone of good character, who will be something in their life. Remember, your families history, values and image are on show for all to see in coming generations. So remember, if you don't stand for something, you'll fall for anything!"

MOTHER TERESA OF CALCUTTA
YUGOSLAV-BORN MISSIONARY

"If you judge people, you have no time to love them."

How often do we hear people making quick judgements of other people? We are all, I would think, guilty of this crime sometimes or even often.

It's easy isn't it to "pidgeon-hole" people and pin a label on them.

It happens all too often in life, business and sport.

For example, "nicknames" are often a form of judgement of someone, and often when used in anger are unkind and show a lack of love.

EPICTETUS
STOIC PHILOSOPHER

"If you hear that someone is speaking ill of you, instead of trying to defend yourself, you should say: he obviously does not know me very well, since there are so many other faults he could have mentioned."

It is not easy at the time to think like this when a so called friend or loved one is speaking badly about you, in your circle of friends and colleagues. However, its motivating, refreshing and grounding to keep things in perspective and have a laugh at yourself.

You'll be the winner then!

ABRAHAM LINCOLN
PRESIDENT OF THE UNITED STATES

**"He has the right to criticise,
who has a heart to help."**

It's a position or situation that coaches, captains, leaders and managers have to deal with in everyday life, sport and business.

Dr John Gray in his best selling book *Men are from Mars, Women are from Venus* in fact, made the point that women especially, don't like or want advice unless they ask for it, because they feel it is being critical of them.

Wow – us men only think we're helping?

JOHN RUSKIN
ENGLISH AUTHOR AND ART CRITIC

"Curiosity is a gift, a capacity of pleasure in knowing, which if you destroy, you make yourselves cold and dull."

Are you adventurous and curious? Do you seek so you shall find? Remember, if you want to gain knowledge, you must be curious and inquisitive.

In fact, with the speed of change in the world at present, not being able to be graphically drawn, it is now a pre-requisite to have an appetite for knowledge to not only be successful but just to survive!

So cultivate your curiosity quickly.

SMILEY BLANTON
AMERICAN MUSICIAN

"A sense of curiosity is nature's original school of education."

When I am coaching a client, I inevitably receive information about an issue or problem that the client has or is experiencing.

I observe that the client consistently, in early sessions, becomes angry or emotional about these issues or problems and finds it very frustrating that they cannot control or solve the position or problem easily.

I, therefore, have to help them to become curious and look for the root causes so they can better understand the reasons and solve the problem or issue themselves.

ALBERT EINSTEIN
GERMAN-BORN AMERICAN PHYSICIST

"The important thing is not to stop questioning."

It is wonderful to see young children all of a sudden, flick the switch and become inquisitive and curious to find out the answer to the three-letter word:
w-h-y?

The challenge in life though, is to maintain the focus and continue to not accept, what you see or hear, but to continually ask – why is it so?

You'll be the wiser and remember, as Peter Drucker, the US management guru once said,
"Knowledge is power!"

CANON HENRY SCOTT-HOLLAND
BRITISH CLERIC

**"Death is nothing at all; does not count.
I have only slipped away into the next room."**

Death is not a topic any of us talk about easily,
but it is a topic or a thought that grips you
suddenly when you go into hospital for
a major operation or treatment.

I confronted my fear seven years ago by putting
my life in the hands of the team at Cabrini Hospital
when I had open-heart surgery.

I told myself they knew what to do,
because I didn't!

SAMUEL JOHNSON
ENGLISH CRITIC AND WRITER

"It matters not how a man dies, but how he lives. The act of dying is not of importance, it lasts so short a time."

Do you fear death? I guess we all do. In fact, it strikes at your very core, your heart, your mind, your emotions and your spirit.

As we become older, it's inevitable that we become involved with the topic more deeply and personally.

However, there has been a positive shift in society and funerals are now being conducted by celebrating more how a person lived not died!

DOLORES IBARRURI
SPANISH COMMUNIST LEADER AND ORATOR

"It is better to die on your feet than live on your knees."

The profession of selling in Australia has grown up and matured over the past 20 years.

No longer is a salesperson a person who simply stands on their feet to push products, but now is considered a relationship building specialist, who researches prospects and empathetically helps them to buy what's best for them.

Those people who don't fit this profile of the modern salesperson have therefore been forced to change their jobs to one that better suits their personality and skills.

ELISABETH KUBLER-ROSS
SWISS-BORN AMERICAN PSYCHIATRIST

"Death can show us the way, for when we know and understand completely that our time on this earth is limited, and that we have no way of knowing when it will be over, then we must live each day as if it were the only one we had."

This is exactly what generations X and Y are doing today.

It's a good lesson to observe because today people no longer feel secure that they can store their wealth like squirrels for the winter – because their winter might never come!

SOCRATES
GREEK PHILOSOPHER

"To fear death, gentlemen, is nothing other than to think oneself wise when one is not; for it is to think one knows what one does not know. No man knows whether death may not even turn out to be the greatest of blessings for a human being; and yet people fear it as if they knew for certain that it is the greatest of evils."

Profound words from a great thinker.
Words that make you think beyond the normal horizon we see each day in life.

WILLIAM PENN
ENGLISH QUAKER AND FOUNDER OF PENNSYLVANIA, USA

"Death is but crossing the world, as friends do the seas; they live in one another still."

It's interesting to think and reflect about the impact and influence we leave on one another.

We now travel the world very easily and have the ability to make friends in so many places.

In fact a friend of mine met a couple in America last year and they surprisingly sent him an e-mail a month ago inviting him and his wife to join them on a cruise around Europe!

PHILIP LARKIN
ENGLISH POET

"What will survive of us is love."

When you're gone from the world, have you stopped to consider what you will be remembered for by the people you have left behind.

Will you be remembered for your wealth, your buildings, your home, your car, your yacht, your work, your sporting achievements or your business success? Perhaps, you will be remembered for your style, your personality, your voice, your writing, your painting, or even, your humour and storytelling.

Well, who knows what, but I'll bet you'll be remembered most for your love, your nature and your character.

ALBERT SCHWEITZER
ALSATIAN MEDICAL MISSIONARY

"Thinking about death ... produces love for life. When we are familiar with death, we accept each week, each day, as a gift. Only if we are able thus to accept life – bit by bit – does it become precious."

Do you have a love for life? Even when we are going through tough economic times, it is useful to treasure life and try to keep things in perspective.

You can't change the world, you can only change and adjust yourself and the way you think and live in the world.

MARY ANN EVANS
KNOWN AS GEORGE ELIOT, ENGLISH NOVELIST

"The years seem to rush by now, and I think of death as a fast approaching end of a journey – double and treble the reason for loving as well as working while it is day."

When friends are approaching the end of their journey do you treat it as a wake up call to love life and especially love what you're doing at work.

We all take life for granted and think it will go on forever, well it won't.

So, make your life count now!

ELISABETH KUBLER-ROSS
AMERICAN PSYCHIATRIST

"Death is the final stage of growth in this life. There is no total death. Only the body dies. The self or spirit, or whatever you may wish to label it, is eternal."

When a loved one passes, it's easy to worry they will be forgotten. Well, it's refreshing to know that you will always experience milestones. For instance, today I am looking at a building where a special friend once lived.

Janet Hider-Smith was a champion glider pilot and a champion friend.

SAMUEL BUTLER
ENGLISH WRITER AND SATIRIST

"To die completely, a person must not only forget but be forgotten, and he who is not forgotten is not dead."

Memories are powerful motivators.
Do you cultivate your memories
and inspire yourself with their message?
Memories are often useful in a range of ways.

They can help you with a solution. They can give you a new direction. They can remind you of important information. They can give you a renewed focus. They can generate excitement and energy and especially they can help you remember a friend.

AGNES DE MILLE
AMERICAN CHOREOGRAPHER

"No trumpets sound when the important decisions of our life are made. Destiny is made known silently."

Usually you don't realise it at the time, but often an important decision about your destiny is made at a time of crisis. Your emotions are in charge at the time and you're often feeling down or even depressed.

Often you're feeling guilty about why something has happened, your pride is taking a battering, and you even think your image is being tarnished.

Don't worry its' just your destiny being fashioned.

PETER DRUCKER
AMERICAN MANAGEMENT CONSULTANT

"Whenever you see a successful business, someone once made a courageous decision."

It's easy to forget isn't it, but most businesses started from a courageous decision.

Today's youth, and even the union movement, sometimes forget that someone actually started BHP, Ford, Coles, Woolworths, Ripcurl, Microsoft, Apple and even Disneyland. Now they employ thousands of people and enable them, and their families, to live a lifestyle that's expected to continue forever.

Well, perhaps we should show more respect for the courage the founder showed in the first place.

THOMAS CARLYLE
SCOTTISH ESSAYIST, HISTORIAN AND PHILOSOPHER

"Our grand business in life is not to see what lies dimly at a distance, but to do what lies clearly at hand."

Do you keep your feet on the ground or are you living in the clouds with as they say, "Delusions of grandeur?"

It's fine to have a vision, but don't only look at the horizon.

If you want to succeed in life, you need to also focus on doing the boring, or the mundane, tasks that enable you to travel to your destination.

ALBERT SCHWEITZER
ALSATIAN MEDICAL MISSIONARY

"A man can only do what he can do. But if he does that each day he can sleep at night and do it again the next day."

Are you proud and satisfied with your working effort each day?

If you answered "yes", well done! If you answered "no" then perhaps you should take time out and assess what it is you are doing and what your passion factor is in doing it.

It's important to respect what you do, but it's also important to love what you do.

EMILY DICKINSON
AMERICAN POET

"A deed knocks first at thought and then – it knocks at will – that is the manufacturing spot."

How often have you thought of doing a good deed or just a deed only to lack the will and sense of urgency to carry the thought through and make it happen?

Deeds can be momentous or just thoughtful, but rest assured they could be significant in the eyes of another.

The key to making them happen is to have the will, desire and commitment to achieve and make someone happy or proud.

MARY ANN EVANS
KNOWN AS GEORGE ELIOT, ENGLISH NOVELIST

"Our deeds travel with us from afar, and what we have been makes us what we are."

Are you proud of the achievements and deeds you have undertaken and accomplished in your life so far? If not, why not, because they travel with you as a part of your baggage or character.

Having a realisation of the significance of deeds you achieve in your life can, and does, shape the perception of how people see you and relate to you through their eyes.

And remember, perception is reality!

KAHLIL GIBRAN
LEBANESE WRITER, ARTIST AND MYSTIC

"Every thought I have imprisoned in expression I must free by my deeds."

In other words, as I would say, "Talk is cheap and deeds are valuable."

It's easy to think your thoughts but difficult to have the courage to express them when the opportunity presents itself. This often happens, at club or group meetings, when a difficult or contentious topic is on the agenda for discussion.

Many people just sit in the audience, think their views, and therefore miss the opportunity to make their contribution for a solution.

HENRY WARD BEECHER
AMERICAN CLERGYMAN

**"Do not be afraid of defeat.
You are never so near victory as
when defeated in a good cause."**

In other words have the courage of your convictions
and be positive in your efforts
to win for a good cause.

Don't let defeat enter your thinking or you can
easily lose your focus, process, plan and position.

It often seems to happen now in AFL football when
a team, which is leading, tries to run the clock down
with about five minutes to play and loses the game.

CHARLES EDWARD MONTAGUE
ENGLISH NOVELIST AND ESSAYIST

"Among the mind's powers is one that comes of itself to many children and artists. It need not be lost, to the end of his days, by anyone who has ever had it. This is the power of taking delight in a thing, or rather in anything, not as a means to some other end, but just because it is what it is. A child in the full health of his mind will put his hand flat on the summer lawn, feel it, and give a little shiver of private glee at the elastic firmness of the globe."

Yes, it once felt delightful.

MICHELANGELO
ITALIAN SCULPTOR, PAINTER AND POET

"Lord, grant that I may always desire more than I can accomplish."

What an insightful comment and one that no doubt moved him to achieve artistic greatness.

It is akin to how champion athletes at the Olympic games think and perform to enable them to perform at their best.

The winners, for example, don't run *to* the tape in a race, but ensure that they are running at their maximum *through* the tape.

PLATO
ANCIENT GREEK PHILOSOPHER

"Desires are only the lack of something: and those who have the greatest desires are in a worse condition than those who have none, or very slight ones."

If you are continually longing for something special in your life, chances are you are not being as productive as you could be.

Remember, "Actions speak louder than words".

However, it's important to realise that action and achievement are evidence that you are industrious and progressive and therefore not in need of always wanting to want something you don't have.

BENEDICT SPINOZA
DUTCH PHILOSOPHER

"Desire is the very essence of man."

Are you content with your success in life, business or sport?

It seems, from my experience, that when you become satisfied with your level of achievement that, in fact, you have taken your eye off the ball and perhaps become complacent.

I remember asking an AFL football coach I was mentoring, with eight matches to go in the season, how he thought his team was performing.

"We're on top and cruising!" he said. Well his team never won another game that season.

THOMAS FULLER
ENGLISH DIVINE AND HISTORIAN

"It is always darkest just before the day dawneth."

If you are experiencing a rough or tough time, remember, "Like the drunk who wakes up, you can only feel better".

In other words, you will often experience events and circumstances that seem dire and you might even want to give up.

Well, don't despair, hang in there and believe in yourself, and your ability to survive the current turmoil in your life, so you can prosper again.

ROGER W. BABSON
AMERICAN ECONOMIST

"When we are flat on our backs there is no way to look but up."

How apt for the economic turmoil of today, but don't despair. Sure there may be some hardship and some tightening of your budget, but you might as well be positive, look up and perhaps change.

For example, with the cost of cigarettes burning a hole in your pocket, what a great time to create a plan to break the habit, give up and get healthy.

Imagine how much better you'll feel and how much money you'll save.

ALBERT CAMUS
FRENCH WRITER

"In the midst of winter, I finally learned that there was in me an invincible summer."

When all is falling about you remember you have more strength than you think.

It is in times of trouble that you must not despair, but show your courage, resilience and cunning to overcome the odds.

However, do this in the knowledge that the sun will shine again with the warmth to help you be happy again. Even the birds and animals show these traits in overcoming the incredible odds of seasons and nature.

WILLIAM ELLERY CHANNING
AMERICAN MINISTER

"To live content with small means; to seek elegance rather than luxury, and refinement rather than fashion; to be worthy, not respectable, and wealthy, not rich; to study hard, think quietly, talk gently, act frankly; to listen to stars and birds, to babes and sages, with open heart; to bear all cheerfully, do all bravely, await occasions, hurry never. In a word to let the spiritual, unbidden and unconscious, grow up through the common. This is to be my symphony."

A great formula for a life of balance!

DANTE ALIGHIERI
ITALIAN POET, STATESMAN AND DIPLOMAT

"If thou follow thy star, thou canst not fail of a glorious haven."

You've heard no doubt of following a hunch or having a sixth sense. Well it's true, if you follow your star you will reach your gold at the end of the rainbow.

However, don't let anyone get in your way or put you off your course.

Be very focussed and committed and stay on track no matter what barriers are put in your way.

It's only those of you who believe in your destiny that will really succeed.

AMBROSE BIERCE
AMERICAN JOURNALIST

"Destiny: a tyrant's excuse for crime and a fool's excuse for failure."

Some people don't believe in destiny, but I do. It's what you do with what you've got, that you do with total passion and commitment, that creates your destiny.

So if you don't have a dominant goal you'll just wander through life and be the classic under-achiever.

But don't panic, many successful people didn't have a goal in their youth. It was only in later life that they saw the benefit of knowing where they wanted to go.

WILLIAM JENNINGS BRYAN
AMERICAN LAWYER AND POLITICIAN

"Destiny is not a matter of chance, it is a matter of choice."

Today you have the opportunity to take charge of your life and make something of it that will make you proud.

Remember, as a saying I have in my office says, "If it is to be, it's up to me".

It's easy to sit back and wait for success to happen, but those of you who achieve your goals will be the ones who create their own luck and their own destiny.

MARCUS AURELIUS
ROMAN EMPEROR AND PHILOSPHER

"Everything that happens happens as it should, and if you observe carefully, you will find this to be so."

The key to achieving your goals in life, business and sport is just this – your powers of observation. For example, if you're early for an appointment or you're kept waiting, observe the way the foyer is presented and maintained and take the opportunity to read any company booklet.

Watch the performance, grooming and attitude of the receptionist and listen. This knowledge can be vital in helping your visit be successful.

BENJAMIN DISRAELI
ENGLISH STATESMAN AND WRITER

"We are not creatures of circumstance; we are creators of circumstance."

It's easy to wait for your luck to change, but it's those of you who take the bull by the horns and turn your luck around that will be the winners.

The key ingredient in being able to do this is to tackle the problem or issues with the right attitude. Once you have an attitude that's positive and shows strong self-belief you will be on the way to achieving your goals and your destiny.

THOMAS FULLER
ENGLISH DIVINE AND HISTORIAN

"All things are difficult before they are easy."

Life, business and sport is often likened to skiing. In life, we often have to go through hard tough times in order to learn and experience failure before we can become successful.

In business, we often have to struggle early before we can become successful later.

In sport, we need to be committed, disciplined and focussed in our development years in order to succeed in our prime years.

Remember, in skiing you need to climb the mountain before you can ski down it.

JOHN BUNYAN
ENGLISH WRITER AND MORALIST

"The hill, though high, I covet to ascend; the difficulty will not offend, for I perceive the way to life lies here. Come, pluck up heart, let's neither faint nor fear; better, though difficult, the right way to go, than wrong, though easy, where the end is woe."

In life your have to be prepared to show courage and do many things without fear or favour.

However, this type of courage is not easy to muster, as often, you will be confronted with an alternate downside as a consequence.

WILLIAM JAMES
AMERICAN PSYCHOLOGIST AND PHILOSOPHER

"Keep the faculty of effort alive in you by a little gratuitous exercise every day. That is be systematically heroic in little unnecessary points, do every day or two something for no other reason than its difficulty."

Great advice for those of you who have recently retired.

It is all too easy to turn off, vegetate and lose the mental edge you once had when working.

Well remember you'll live longer, keep your friends together and keep your marriage together too, if you keep challenging yourself and stretching your mind.

WILLIAM SHAKESPEARE
ENGLISH PLAYWRIGHT AND POET

**"Determine on some course,
more than a wild exposure to each chance."**

Do you make career goals, write shopping lists and plan your holidays or do you just let them happen.

Chances are you will therefore not achieve as much in your career as you could and, in addition, you will buy more than you need when shopping.

You will also not take advantage of the best deals in air travel, sea travel or accommodation and find it difficult to save.

So get more organised and you will be the winner.

VINCENT VAN GOGH
DUTCH POST-IMPRESSIONIST PAINTER

"The thing has already taken form in my mind before I start it. The first attempts are absolutely unbearable. I say this because I want you to know that if you see something worthwhile in what I am doing, it is not by accident but because of real direction and purpose."

Are you the artist in your business, setting the scene and direction in your mind or are you simply throwing paint at the canvas hoping it will stick and that you'll be successful in the end?

GEORGE WASHINGTON
THE FIRST PRESIDENT OF THE UNITED STATES

"Discipline is the soul of an army. It makes small numbers formidable, procures success to the weak, and esteem to all."

I have observed that people who are poor time managers lack discipline to be good ones.

They take on too many tasks, try to please too many people, try to fit too much into their day, and rarely use a diary.

However, the biggest issue I see they have, is that deep down they don't really respect other people and their time enough in the first place.

MARCEL PROUST
FRENCH NOVELIST

**"The real voyage of discovery consists
not in seeking new landscapes
but in having new eyes."**

The way you look at new opportunities can often be
the difference between success and failure.

It's similar to the way you look at problems in life by
seeing things from another point of view.

We all have the power to choose how we look
at things and either, take the positive view
or the negative.

So if you want your life to take a turn for the better
look at it through positive eyes.

ALBERT SZENT-GYÖRGYI
HUNGARIAN-BORN AMERICAN BIOCHEMIST

"Discovery consists of seeing what everybody has seen and thinking what nobody has thought."

I guess it's like the well-known adage in life, business and sport that you are silly doing the same things over, and over again and expecting a difference outcome!

If you want to discover a new solution then you need to not follow the crowd and instead be your own person. It is easy to always get caught in the trap of thinking as we always think which we think is normal. The key to discovery is to think differently from a new perspective.

WOODROW WILSON
FORMER PRESIDENT OF THE UNITED STATES

"All big men are dreamers. They see things in the soft haze of a spring day or in the red fire of a long winter's evening. Some of us let great dreams die, but others nourish and protect them, nurse them through bad days till they bring them to the sunshine and light which comes always to those who sincerely hope that their dreams will come true."

It really hurts, doesn't it, to think of an idea or solution, not write it down and watch someone else do it.

GEORGE BERNARD SHAW
IRISH DRAMATIST, ESSAYIST AND CRITIC

"Some men see things as they are and say 'why?' I dream things that never were, and say, 'why not?'"

The challenge in life is not to follow others like sheep. Today, more than ever, it is important to challenge the status quo and not be lulled into a false sense of security.

Therefore, have the courage of your convictions, question the issue, and say what you think.

Not only will others envy you but also you will be admired for your initiative.

HENRY DAVID THOREAU
AMERICAN ESSAYIST, POET AND MYSTIC

"Go confidently in the direction of your dreams! Live the life you've imagined."

Many famous people throughout history have dreamt of the life they achieved when they were young. There are many examples of this and one that comes to mind is Li Cunxin, author of *Mao's Last Dancer*. He was born to bitter poverty but dreamed of being the best dancer in China. He trained and danced for the Houston Ballet and was Principal dancer with the Australian Ballet while studying accounting and finance. He is now a successful stockbroker.

The key is to confidently believe in yourself.

HENRY DAVID THOREAU
AMERICAN ESSAYIST, POET AND MYSTIC

"If you have built castles in the air, your work need not be lost; that is where they should be. Now put the foundations under them."

Successful people in history have dared to dream. do you dream? Well, making your dreams come true is another achievement in itself?

It's like creating a building. Architects see the finished vision in their mind and graphically on paper but the engineers convert this vision to reality by completing computations and calculations, which enable the building to rise to complete the vision.

GURU RHH

"Take your dream, attach it to a star and never lose it. If you lose it ... you've lost your enthusiasm; you've settled for something less. This will never do. Fight like hell for your dream and get it."

It is easy when you dream or create a eureka, or great idea, to have your spirit and enthusiasm quickly dampen by others you share it with.

Don't let this happen to you because others do not have the same courage or level of enthusiasm as you have, to make your dreams come true.

THOMAS LOVELL BEDDOES
ENGLISH POET AND PHYSIOLOGIST

"If there were dreams to sell, what would you buy? Some cost a passing-bell; some a light sigh."

Have you noticed that when you come up with great ideas they are often met with varying degrees of enthusiasm? Well don't be disappointed if they don't all receive the recognition they deserve.

Remember, everyone has a different perception of an idea depending on how you sell it. Some people identify easily with your thoughts and are instantly interested, while others will simply sigh and show a level of indifference.

EDGAR ALLAN POE
AMERICAN POET AND WRITER

"Those who dream by day are cognizant of many things which escape those who dream only by night."

It's often considered a waste of time to be a day dreamer, but those who dream by day will usually consider more things more carefully and even remember them!

The important thing to do to bring them to reality, is to jot down as many thoughts as you can whilst they are happening. Then put them in a place, for future reference, which I often call the parking lot of life.

HENRY DAVID THOREAU
AMERICAN ESSAYIST, POET AND MYSTIC

"Dreams are the touchstones of our characters."

What will motivate you to achieve your goals in life?

An event, a friend, a colleague, a member of your family or simply yourself. Then why not give yourself the opportunity to explore your dreams and develop your future.

Remember, it's never too late to take action and make your dreams come true.

You just have to take a big breath, believe in your plan and focus on putting it into action. However, the hardest part is starting.

ELEANOR ROOSEVELT
FIRST LADY OF THE UNITED STATES

"The future belongs to those who believe in the beauty of their dreams."

Barack Obama, when campaigning to become the 44th president of the United States, gave the world a glimpse of his passion and belief in the beauty of his dreams.

Not only did he eloquently express his beliefs and his feelings, but also you could feel by the grandness of his oratory, that he knew he belonged in the role and that the people wanted him to lead them into the challenging yet exciting future of their country.

CARL JUNG
SWISS PSYCHIATRIST

**"Who looks outside dreams;
who looks inside wakes."**

In other words, we are all creatures of habit and do things like a robot everyday.

The key to realising your full potential is to look outside the norm and dream. It's why using your imagination and creative thinking is so important to enable growth.

You have no doubt in recent years heard the expression to "think outside the square", well this saying originated from people thinking in a new or lateral way which contravened convention and enabled them to dream.

T.E. LAWRENCE
(KNOWN AS LAWRENCE OF ARABIA).
ENGLISH SOLDIER AND WRITER

"All men dream, but not equally. Those who dream by night in the dusty recesses of their minds wake in the day to find that it was vanity: but the dreamers of the day are dangerous men, for they may act their dream with open eyes, to make it possible."

Dreaming in the day, I believe,
could perhaps be better described
as planning and thinking strategically.

The most successful leaders in business,
life and sport make this a normal
part of enabling them to succeed.

MARY SHELLEY
ENGLISH AUTHOR

"My dreams were all my own; I accounted for them to nobody; they were my refuge when annoyed – my dearest pleasure when free."

Authors are interesting and often very private people. I guess I know.

They find their dreams are often their inspiration for their work, but they keep them private and store them up as ideas, like squirrels store nuts for food.

In other words, dreams for authors are like a storage of ideas, themes, plots and characters and they are kept private as in a vault – because to them they are very precious.

ANNE FARADAY
AMERICAN PSYCHOLOGIST AND DREAM RESEARCHER

"Learning to understand our dreams is a matter of learning to understand our heart's language."

In other words, dreams are the language of the heart and, as we know, the heart seems to think in emotional ways, whereas the head seems to think in more logical ways.

It therefore seems to make sense that when we dream we are talking to ourselves emotionally and trying to leave a message of future action or an opportunity. Have you ever experienced something or taken an action and thought "you'd done it before!"

G.K. CHESTERTON
ENGLISH WRITER

"Education is simply the soul of a society as it passes from one generation to another."

Generational change is with us all and it's interesting when you're a parent or grandparent to see this happening in front of your eyes.

The interesting thing though, is that because of the emotional involvement that consumes us during this time, we often are not conscious of what is really happening.

It sort of happens by stealth. So next time you're with your children or grandchildren, stop and take in the transferring of knowledge in real time.

RUBY MANIKAN
INDIAN CHURCH LEADER

"If you educate a man you educate a person, but if you educate a women you educate a family."

How true, but today this thought might be taken as sexist by a large percentage of our society.

Women in the family, however, still play an important, vital and influential role in influencing the education, values and therefore standards of the family. In fact, this comment makes me think and become more aware of the respect, recognition and reward that society needs to show to women in the education of a family.

MARCUS AURELIUS
ROMAN EMPEROR AND PHILOSOPHER

"Nothing happens to any man that he is not formed by nature to bear."

Yes, men and women are magnificent machines, capable of supreme endurance and achievement. Men, for example are designed with great strength of limb, whereas women are designed with great strength of mind.

Both assets provide great endurance and the ability for man to have physical power whilst women, I observe, to have emotional power.

It is often said, in life, business and in sport, that "there is a strong-minded woman behind every successful man!"

HELEN KELLER
AMERICAN LECTURER, WRITER AND SCHOLAR

"We could never learn to be brave and patient if there were only joy in the world."

It's true that if we only experienced joy, we would not be equipped for the full, expansive journey of life.

Hardship, disaster, loss, distress and sadness, I guess, are all reasons or events in life that help to shape your skills, endurance and character.

These unhappy experiences therefore enable you to acquire, hone and increase your knowledge and skills and round you off with "a finishing school for life!"

WILLIAM PENN
ENGLISH QUAKER AND FOUNDER OF PENNSYLVANIA, USA

"No pain, no palm; no thorns, no throne; no gall, no glory; no cross, no crown."

In reality, you have to do the hard yards or time in life to reap the reward of the good times. Two world celebrities in sport and journalism, Gary Player and Michael Parkinson, have revealed, when interviewed, that their fathers were both miners who worked hard and "broke their back" for their family.

Witnessing the hard work and conditions in which they worked drove these celebrities to work hard and excel at their careers.

VIRGIL
ROMAN POET

"Endure, and keep yourself for days of happiness."

Are you aware of the importance of this profound statement? In other words, plan to keep yourself fit in body, mind and spirit in times of unhappiness or ill health, so you enjoy and take advantage of the happiness that will eventually come your way.

It's easy to feel down and even depressed when things are not going your way and you need a plan and a process to help you stay positive.

So remind yourself often so you are ready for the good times!

CHARLES HADDON SPURGEON
ENGLISH CLERGYMAN

**"Beware of no man more than yourself;
we carry our worst enemies within us."**

Probably the greatest enemies we carry within us
are self-belief and confidence.

Our upbringing in our formative years is often
the biggest influence on these aspects.

It's also how we react to peer group pressure that
affects us. I believe it's these enemies that
motivate young people to feel the need to start
smoking cigarettes or try drugs. We are all fragile
beings so we need to have a strategy to fight
these enemies within and win.

WILLIAM JAMES
AMERICAN PSYCHOLOGIST AND PHILOSOPHER

"If an unusual necessity forces us onward, a surprising thing occurs. The fatigue gets worse up to a certain point, when, gradually or suddenly, it passes away and we are fresher than before! We have evidently tapped a new level of energy. There may be layer after layer of this experience, a third and fourth wind. We find amounts of ease and power that we never dreamed ourselves to own, sources of strength habitually not taxed, because habitually we never push through the obstruction of fatigue."

So push yourself again and again and win.

JOHN BARRYMORE
AMERICAN ACTOR

**"He neither drank, smoked, nor rode a bicycle.
Living frugally, saving his money, he died
early surrounded by greedy relatives.
It was a great lesson to me."**

In today's economic turmoil it's easy to justify
becoming frugal, negative and scared.

However, in times of hardship it's also necessary
to maintain a positive outlook and your network of
friends. Putting yourself in too much isolation also
puts you at risk of becoming depressed
and anxious.

So each day try to look on the bright side of life and
remember to celebrate how lucky you are.

RALPH WALDO EMERSON
AMERICAN ESSAYIST, POET AND PHILOSOPHER

"Nothing great was ever achieved without enthusiasm."

I have met many people during my life and have observed a common thread amongst those who achieved success.

Each one of these people I felt had the vital ingredient, trait or spark of enthusiasm. This special gift separates the mediocre from the excellent, the ordinary from the special, and the unsuccessful from the successful.

So when in doubt take a risk, speak up, take action, be confident, step outside your comfort zone and show your enthusiasm to the world.

HENRY DAVID THOREAU
AMERICAN POET, ESSAYIST AND MYSTIC

"None so old as those who have outlived enthusiasm."

Retirement is looked forward to by many people, but when they get there; they are often disappointed, disillusioned and distressed.

I meet many retired executives who find their new life lonely, boring, mundane and lacking in vibrance. The satisfaction and reward they once had, together with the enthusiastic, mental stimulation, seems to have vanished. As a result, they grow old fast and their health and mind deteriorates before your eyes. So plan your life to remain mentally and physically active.

NORMAL VINCENT PEALE
AMERICAN WRITER AND MINISTER

"If you are not getting as much from life as you want to, then examine the state of your enthusiasm."

Are you happy with your lot in life?
If not, stop and take stock of yourself!

Chances are you're not letting yourself "free wheel" and therefore not reaping the rewards of your efforts. Often we are too careful and always worrying about making mistakes.

If this is you, then review your life, do an assessment and I'm sure you will find that you are "living with the brakes on!"

DALE CARNEGIE
AMERICAN AUTHOR AND LECTURER

"Act enthusiastic and you become enthusiastic."

However, before you can become enthusiastic you need to set the goals you want to achieve.

For example, do you want to lower your golf handicap, improve your serve in tennis, become the skipper of your bowls team or enter a fun run?

Perhaps you want to learn to paint, build, learn a new language, cook, become a better photographer or start your own business. Whatever it is, set your goals first and then you will more likely throw yourself into achieving them.

HENRY FORD
AMERICAN CAR MANUFACTURER

"You can do anything if you have enthusiasm ... enthusiasm is at the bottom of all progress. With it, there is accomplishment. Without it, there are only alibis."

Is the consistent, negative, bad news in the newspaper, on the radio and on the television pouring cold water on your plans to grow. Well stop thinking this negative way and instead start thinking in a more positive way.

Change your environment and listen to beautiful music, watch funny television and read a positive book.

Don't make excuses for yourself.

SAMUEL GOLDWYN
AMERICAN FILM PRODUCER

"No man who is enthusiastic about his work has anything to fear from life."

There is no question, that from my experiences in life, as a coach and mentor, that a man's success in life stems from his success in his work.

Enthusiasm, it also appears, is the necessary ingredient in order for work to be successful. It's what's necessary for the circle of life and I think this also relates strongly to the saying, "Success breeds success".

So, approach what you do with enthusiasm, and you will reap the rewards of success.

FRANCOIS PIERRE GUILLAUME GUIZOT
FRENCH HISTORIAN AND STATESMAN

"Do not be afraid of enthusiasm. You need it. You can do nothing effectively without it."

It is interesting to observe, how many people are scared of showing their enthusiasm when working on a project that they love. Why is this? Are you frightened to be yourself, scared of what people might think, or is it your lack of confidence showing through.

Well, trust your judgement and let your emotions show, and don't be afraid of what others might think.

They just might catch your enthusiasm too.

SAMUEL JOHNSON
ENGLISH CRITIC AND WRITER

"The love of life is necessary to the vigorous prosecution of any understanding."

In today's "bad news world" it's easy to find yourself feeling down or even depressed.

Well remember, the news media only feeds you bad news, because they know that's what sells newspapers and advertising.

The trick is to put *all* the bad news you are fed in context and keep your life balanced and calm. So, why not listen to music and relax. You'll be better for the experience and so will your family.

CHARLES KINGSLEY
ENGLISH WRITER AND CLERGYMAN

"We act as though comfort and luxury were the chief requirements of life, when all that we need to make us really happy is something to be enthusiastic about."

Have you noticed that when you embark on a new project, trip, or job that you become happy and excited.

You can be down in the dumps one day and on top of the world the next.

Well, if you want to experience the highs more often, be prepared to try something new in your life.

BOOKER TALIAFERIO WASHINGTON
AMERICAN TEACHER, WRITER AND SPEAKER,

"Excellence is to do a common thing in an uncommon way."

Excellence is a well-used word, but it's not a well-performed trait. You experience people every day thinking they are trying to be excellent, but really only being mediocre.

You see it's really easy to be mediocre or ordinary in life, business or sport, but really hard to be excellent.

Striving for excellence requires a mindset, a plan and a process, but above all, it requires belief in your goal and pride in yourself.

BENJAMIN FRANKLIN
AMERICAN STATESMAN AND PHILOSOPHER

"He that is good at making excuses is seldom good at anything else."

Do you take responsibility for your actions or do you always make excuses if you let people down or fail?

Chances are if you continually make excuses you are not only kidding yourself, but encouraging a bad habit to develop.

Being responsible and accountable for yourself and your actions takes courage and bravery, but it is also training yourself to be honest and transparent with yourself. So, make a habit of assessing your efforts honestly.

ERICA JONG
AMERICAN NOVELIST AND POET

"The trick is not how much pain you feel – but how much joy you feel. Any idiot can feel pain. Life is full of excuses to feel pain, excuses not to live, excuses, excuses, excuses."

Do you wallow in self-pity instead of taking responsibility for yourself and training your brain to focus on the joy and good you can create and the good things in your life.

If you do then there is a good way to try and overcome these negative feelings. It's called daily positive self-talk and it really works!

ALDOUS HUXLEY
ENGLISH NOVELIST AND ESSAYIST

"Experience is not what happens to a man. It is what a man does with what happens to him."

Have you ever reflected on a hurtful experience and come to realise that it was how you reacted to a certain person or situation and not what they or that did to you?

It's a form of blame where you don't want to take responsibility for your actions, feelings or response.

In fact, it's easy to let other people's actions trick you into thinking it was all their fault and that you were blameless.

JOHN KEATS
POET

"Nothing ever becomes real till it is experienced. Even a proverb is no proverb to you till your life has illustrated it."

In other words, as I often say, talk is cheap. As you have probably heard often, "Actions speak louder than words". In business, this has never been so true and managers, supervisors and staff are forever receiving complaints of poor customer experiences and showing their frustration with policies, processes and procedures. Well, a good way to check whether these are appropriate is to often become a customer of your own business and experience your own businesses performance.

ALFRED, LORD TENNYSON
ENGLISH POET

"And other's follies teach us not, nor much their wisdom teaches, and most, of sterling worth, is what our own experience teaches."

In life, business and sport we can be told, shown and educated in many aspects of a skill or a method, but often we will never really believe these words of wisdom until we experience them ourselves.

This experience then not only cements the messages we are given, but often enables us to extend and develop them to make them more real or complete. This is when the real meanings in life hit home and stick.

OSCAR WILDE
IRISH POET, WIT AND DRAMATIST

"Experience is the name everyone gives to their mistakes."

At the time, we don't realise what's happening, but in the end we realise that what we are and what we learn, are the results of events and lessons along the road of life.

So when you're experiencing some mistakes, take heed in the knowledge that one day you'll be the better and wiser for them.

It's often described as attending the university of life and sitting for the most demanding exams to help you grow and develop.

VERNON SANDERS LAW

"Experience is a hard teacher because she gives the test first, the lesson afterwards."

In other words, we have to pass the test of life with all its anguish, anxiety, stress, heartache and often depression and even anger first before we can gain from the lesson.

It's then, and only then, that the lesson with its many messages comes home to you for you to reap the benefits and their rewards for the future.

The key, of course, in learning from these lessons, is to reflect on what you should have done differently.

HERBERT LOUIS SAMUEL
BRITISH POLITICIAN AND ADMINISTRATOR

"The art of living is the art of using experience – your own and other people's."

Do you learn from your past and, more importantly, do you learn from listening and associating with other people? If you do, well done, but if you don't you are missing out on a great opportunity to develop yourself and your life.

It's why many people today in these busy, often stressful times, avail themselves of a mentor.

A mentor can help you learn from their past mistakes and accelerate your growth.

ELIZABETH BOWEN
IRISH NOVELIST

> "Experience isn't interesting till it begins to repeat itself – in fact, till it does that, it hardly *is* experience."

That's probably true, but the only problem is this can reveal that you're not learning from your experience. In business, for instance, a person or the business itself that doesn't make any mistakes is often not moving forward and trying to keep pace with change.

Instead, you and the business could be stuck in a rut, and not thinking or performing differently and creatively in an effort to develop and grow.

OLIVER WENDELL HOLMES
AMERICAN WRITER

"A moment's insight is sometimes worth a life's experience."

Yes it can be, but how do you get them?
Well, wise people ask others questions and listen with interest. Listening, though is an act that not everyone can do well.

Too often, you can become anxious or desperate to impress and talk too much in a conversation.

The gaining of wisdom, however, is usually achieved by listening and gaining insights from people during conversation when you least expect them. They are often called "pearls of wisdom!"

OSCAR WILDE
IRISH POET, WIT AND DRAMATIST

**"Experience is one thing
you can't get for nothing."**

Yes, you can either pay the price for your experience
or you can pay the price of a book, lunch or a
good bottle of wine to gain knowledge from
a friend or mentor.

Today in your stressed, strained world of rush and
bustle, it's a great idea to take the time and trouble
to visit a bookshop and browse. The inquisitive also
call up friends, relatives and colleagues and just
have a drink and a chat.

KATHERINE MANSFIELD
NEW ZEALAND AUTHOR

"When we begin to take our failures non-seriously, it means we are ceasing to be afraid of them. It is of immense importance to learn to laugh at ourselves."

Do you ever think you take yourself too seriously? I did once, but then I changed my outlook and listened to my friends and now I don't.

It's easy to fall for this trait though in times of stress, loneliness, ill health or depression.

However, joining a club is often a great way to help you lighten up, relax and laugh at yourself.

MARGARET H. ALDERSON
JOURNALIST

"If at first you don't succeed you're running about average."

Do you give up the first time you fail? Well, if you do, you will never be successful. In life, business or sport it takes pride in yourself to "bounce back" and try again. In fact, it's a good barometer of your resilience and determination.

In business, research says that 80 percent of business is made on average on the 5th call, but only 20 percent of people make five calls, the others give up. Therefore, 80 percent of business is made by 20 percent of people.

ELBERT HUBBARD
AMERICAN WRITER

"A failure is a man who has blundered, but is not able to cash in on the experience."

People in their own business often make mistakes along the way, but are too emotionally scared to learn from their mistakes and start again.

Yes, I know it's difficult, but the key to starting again is to reflect on your mistake, or mistakes, and analyse what went wrong and why.

Write down the goal you were trying to achieve. chances are your goal was unrealistic.
So, set a new one and try again

CHARLES HADDON SPURGEON
ENGLISH CLERGYMAN

"He who never fails will never grow rich."

How has the year started out for you? Has it been hard to get started because of a failure last year?

Well, it's amazing what can happen when you can put that behind you and start out again.

Write down some new goals, make a plan, talk to some friends and bounce some ideas around. Then go to your wardrobe and put on the clothes that make you feel good. You'll be surprised how your mind, attitude and luck will change.

J. M. BARRIE
SCOTTISH WRITER

> **"We are all of us failures –
> at least the best of us are."**

It seems that the most successful people in life, business and sport are the ones that have suffered the pain of failure on more than one occasion. Failure can act as a motivation and provide you with a reality check.

It's easy to often get ahead of yourself and believe your own PR, but a failure or two quickly brings you back to earth.

So treat your next failure as a chance to show yourself what you're really made of.

GWILYM LLOYD GEORGE
WELSH POLITICIAN

"He's no failure. He's not dead yet."

It's often a sad affair when a person who is successful is not recognised until they have died.

There are many examples of this happening, but I guess one of the most publicised is Heath Ledger who played The Joker in the Batman film *The Dark Knight*.

In fact his performance and therefore the man and the actor, was considered so great he was awarded an Oscar postuimisly for best supporting actor. His fame and talent will now live on in our minds forever.

DINAH MARIA CRAIK
ENGLISH NOVELIST AND POET

"Say not that she did well or ill, only 'she did her best.'"

In life, business and sport, you often get only one chance, one opportunity to achieve your dream. However, don't take it for granted that it will be easy because that's when you will stumble and fail.

James Hird, the Essendon AFL past champion was one of the best prepared footballers to play the game. So was Shane Crawford, the Hawthorn AFL great. They both won Brownlow medals and an AFL premiership too.

ANDRE MAUROIS
FRENCH WRITER

"If men could regard the events of their lives with more open minds they would frequently discover that they did not really desire the things they failed to obtain."

It often happens that you strive to achieve a certain goal, only to come up short. Then you think and ponder what might have been and often come to the conclusion that it wasn't that important afterall.

So the next time you fail in an attempt to win, don't beat yourself up too much and be more philosophical about the result.

SAMUEL SMILES
SCOTTISH AUTHOR AND SOCIAL REFORMER

"We learn wisdom from failure much more than success. We often discover what we *will* do, by finding out what we will *not* do."

The great miler, Herb Herbert, once told me that his success, apart from his athletic ability and fitness, was his intense fear of failure.

In fact he would get so worked up before a race that he would get cramps in the neck and often be physically sick.

His amazing success stemmed from his motivation *not to lose* more than his desire *to win*.

"FREDERIC FARRER"
ENGLISH CLERGYMAN AND WRITER

"There is only one real failure in life that is possible and that is, not to be true to the best one knows."

There are many examples in life, business and sport for you to observe, but one of the best is the great AFL footballer, master coach and legend, Ronald Dale Barassi.

He has always been considered a role model by many people. He told me once that he lived and performed by the motto, "When you get the chance to perform in life bring your best with you".

HENRY WADSWORTH LONGFELLOW
AMERICAN POET

"Be still, sad heart! And cease repining; behind the clouds is the sun still shining; thy fate is the common fate of all, into each life some rain must fall."

Remember, when things are not always going your way to realise that you are experiencing lifes balancing scales at work.

At the time I know you're sad, but keep faith in the knowledge that you're a child of the universe and vunerable to the ups and downs of life. The key often to staying balanced and focussed is to realise just this.

VIRGIL
ROMAN POET

"They can because they think they can."

In today's mostly negative, often depressing and fast paced world, it's important to ensure that you work on your mind as much as your body.

Many people I'm glad to say, today go to a gym, run or walk and watch their diet, but they don't work out with their mind.

As the saying goes, "You are what you think of most of the time". Therefore, today you need to work hard at your mind fitness and believe in yourself more positively, then you will experience success more often.

PEARL S. BUCK
AMERICAN NOVELIST

"I feel no need for any other faith than my faith in human beings."

It's interesting when our children meet their new partner and we are first introduced to their partner's parents and friends. At first we are some what cautious and take our time to come to grips and feel comfortable with new people and their values. Well, it's only human nature at work in its purest form.

You see, it's important to feel comfortable and confident with new friends before you can make a wise decision to trust them, respect them and accept them.

MARTIN LUTHER KING
AMERICAN CIVIL-RIGHTS LEADER

"In the midst of outer dangers I have felt an inner calm and known resources of strength that only god could give. In many instances I have felt the power of god transforming the fatigue of despair into the buoyancy of hope. I am convinced that the universe is under the control of a loving purpose and that in the struggle for righteousness man has cosmic companionship. Behind the harsh appearances of the world there is a benign power."

Perhaps there is real wisdom in his powerful words.

GEORGE SANTAYANA
SPANISH AMERICAN PHILOSOPHER AND POET

"Proof is the last thing looked for by a truly religious mind which feels the imaginative fitness of its faith."

Often you don't want proof to believe in something you emotionally hold very dear. However, this can prove somewhat dangerous in business and can result in blindly following a path, belief or strategy.

So be carful in todays stressful economic climate to check your position and whether you are on the right course or not. Today more than ever, people are not prepared to take uncalculated risks and want to feel in control.

ARTHUR SCHOPENHAUER
PHILOSOPHER

"Whatever fate befalls you, do not give way to great rejoicing, or great lamentation ... All things are full of change, and your fortunes may turn at any moment."

They say life is a balancing act and if you fall off the high wire it's a long way down – but it's easy to over react in life and lose your balance.

The skill is to keep things in perspective.

How often have you celebrated too much before achieving your goal, or as they say in sport – getting ahead of yourself and losing focus.

FRANK MCKINNEY HUBBARD

"Lots of folks confuse bad management with destiny."

It's easy to get down on yourself and start to doubt your ability when in fact the planets, as they say, were just not aligned for you to succeed.

Sometimes things outside your control take over and create situations that just aren't fair. There is often nothing you can do about these circumstances, but the key to survival or success is how you plan and react to the position.

Remember, as the former Australian Prime Minister Malcolm Fraser once said, "Life wasn't meant to be easy".

G.K. CHESTERTON
ENGLISH WRITER

"I do not believe in a fate that falls on men however they act; but I do believe in a fate that falls on them unless they act."

Are you in charge of your destiny or are you letting destiny be in charge of you? To be successful in business or sport it is said you need or must make it happen.

However, in your personal life it is said it is better to let it happen naturally.

This it seems is true when trying to meet a new partner, no matter what your age.

CONFUCIUS
CHINESE PHILOSOPHER

**"When you have faults,
do not fear to abondon them."**

The courageous in the community have the courage
to confront their faults and try and overcome them.
Are you courageous and confront your faults?

In coaching and mentoring I see many clients who
find this, in the early stages, very difficult.

However, when they receive feedback from their
peers this usuallly helps them to realise them and
take action. The key of course is to be brave enough
to admit to them and then work on eliminating them.

BENJAMIN FRANKLIN
FORMER AMERICAN PRESIDENT, STATESMAN AND PHILOSOPHER

> **"Love your enemies,
> for they tell you your faults."**

Feedback is the new term for "constructive criticism" and often your competitors in business are the best source of feedback.

To keep relevant in the marketplace it is vital that you maintain your research and realise what the market thinks of you. Then, and only then can you often hear of your faults and take assertive action to fix them.

This is especially true of political parties who think they are invincible only to find out they are not and lose power.

NORMAN VINCENT PEALE
AMERICAN WRITER AND MINISTER

"Fear is never a reason for quitting: it is only an excuse."

When things don't go your way in life, business and sport, its easy to fear a bad result and give up. It happens especially in sport when a player or a team who has been attacking and playing positively, fears losing and tries not to lose.

They change their mental outlook and therefore their positive skill set and instead become negative and lose their skill set. They either then lose or just fall over the line.

BERTRAND RUSSELL
ENGLISH PHILOSOPHER AND MATHEMATICIAN

"To fear love is to fear life, and those who fear life are already three parts dead."

If you've been hurt in a relationship, it often takes a while for the grief cycle to be completed.

No doubt for a while you might even fear love again and lose trust in others.

The grief cycle is not well known, and consists of 5 stages: *denial, anger, bargaining, depression, acceptance.*

Remember, you will survive, you will heal and you will love again.

RALPH WALDO EMERSON
AMERICAN ESSAYIST, POET AND PHILOSOPHER

"Do the thing you fear and the death of fear is certain."

Many people each year rate the fear of public speaking as their greatest fear in life. If this is your fear there is one good way to overcome it. Do it often!

Remember, that the root cause of why it is a fear is that you are not confident of performing well and the reasons you are not confident are usually the following:

1. You don't *know* your subject.
2. You don't *plan* your speech.
3. You don't *practice* your presentation.

MARIE CURIE
FRENCH PHYSICIST

**"Nothing in life is to be feared.
It is only to be understood."**

Often we need a clearer understanding of life in order to overcome our fear. In business the famous American leadership guru, Peter Druker made famous the statement, "Knowledge is power".

Today in the economic state of the world this has never been more true and important.

If you want to be successful in life, business and sport you must think strategically and plan ahead with the knowledge necessary to enable you and your team to perform at your best.

FRANKLIN D. ROOSEVELT
FORMER PRESIDENT OF THE UNITED STATES

"Let me assert my firm belief that the only things we have to fear is fear itself."

It is said we all have a fear of the unknown. However, the unknown is often a paradise full of dreams and not a negative minefield of pain.

So why do we fear the unknown? Is it the natural tendency to worry about what we can't control or is it the value systems of the environment we live in influencing our thinking.

Whatever it is, try to conquer your fear and think positively.

BERTRAND RUSSELL
ENGLISH PHILOSOPHER AND MATHEMATICIAN

"To conquer fear is the beginning of wisdom, in the pursuit of truth as in the endeavour after a worthy manner of life."

To search for the truth often takes courage, but in the process we can learn valuable messages to give us knowledge and wisdom for the future.

At the time it is easy for fear to take its grip on you, but in the end you'll be the wiser for the effort.

The key to overcoming fear can often simply be the anticipation of a successful outcome.

GERTRUDE STEIN
AMERICAN AUTHOR

"Considering how dangerous everything is nothing is really very frightening."

Often it is said we worry unduly about nothing. All too often we are influenced by others too easily and become worried about things out of all proportion.

The media, if you let them, can too easily influence you into becoming negative and scared. As a consequence its easy to become depressed and disheartened. The economy is a good example of this.

An interesting comment was once made by my accountant when he said, "When they report it it's already happened".

RUDYARD KIPLING
ENGLISH POET AND AUTHOR

"Of all the liars in the world, sometimes the worst are your own fears."

It is easy to trick yourself into fearing the worst when someone takes a certain action. For example, when a manager calls you into their office and asks you to shut the door and take a seat, it seems the automatic reaction is to fear the worst.

In fact managers can often use this strategy as a way of getting an employees attention and focus on a difficult problem so they can make the discussion have impact.

LUCIA CAPACCHIONE
AMERICAN ART THERAPIST AND PIONEER IN INNER HEALING

"When I became ill, the years of pain and confusion loomed up like some primitive monster of the deep. I had to face the monster or drown. There were many nights when I thought I was going under for the last time. I lived in fear of dying. The strange paradox is that by confronting my fear of death, I found myself and created a new life."

Have you confronted your own fears?

When you do, you will discover that you really are the master of your destiny.

JOHN F. KENNEDY
FORMER PRESIDENT OF THE UNITED STATES

**"Forgive your enemies,
but never forget their names."**

It is one of the hardest things to do in life and one that can take a long while to achieve.

To forgive someone who hurts you is not easy, but it is essential to enable you to move on in life.

At the time you can burn inside with rage at their actions, but trying to forgive them will help you to put out the fire of hatred, for that fire can burn you up and even kill you.

CATHERINE PONDER
AMERICAN MOTIVATIONAL WRITER

"The forgiving state of mind is a magnetic power for attracting good. No good thing can be withheld from the forgiving state of mind."

After the grieving process following the death or divorce of a loved one you can either wallow in the wilderness, seek solitude with yourself or explore the unknown for excitement.

The key to coping and moving forward is to forgive the person for their actions.

When you have accomplished this and it may take you quite a while, you will attract other people and the good in yourself will shine.

ALEXANDER POPE
ENGLISH POET

"To err is human, to forgive, divine."

We can all be guilty from time to time of making poor decisions or even stupid ones and it's easy to come down hard on yourself afterwards.

The problem when you do this is that you re inforce to yourself that you are stupid and incompetent, when you are not at all. In fact it's easy to even start believing and acting that way regularly.

This attitude and negative self talk often happens in sport and stops people achieving their true potential.

M. SCOTT PECK
AMERICAN PSYCHIATRIST AND WRITER

"The reason to forgive is for your own sake, for our own health. Because beyond that point needed for healing, if we hold onto our anger, we stop growing and our souls begin to shrivel."

Do you still hold a grudge against someone? Well if you do, try to exorcise it from your mind. You will heal faster, your anger will dissappear quicker and calmness will be restored.

To help you achieve this try to avoid contact with that person or avoid being in their presence.

Remember, time heals.

FRANCOIS DUC DE LA ROCHEFOUCAULD
FRENCH WRITER

"One forgives as much as one loves."

In other words, if you love yourself unconditionally you can forgive others more quickly.

However, this isn't easy when something happens to make you doubt yourself. The key for progress then is to analyse the situation and find out the root cause or causes.

This process is very important in enabling you to put issues and comments into their true perspective. Then you can really see more clearly why things went wrong and work on restoring your self esteem, self love and self confidence.

JEAN-PAUL SARTRE
FRENCH WRITER

"Once freedom lights its beacon in a man's heart, the gods are powerless against him."

Freedom can really set you on a powerful course for success.

Freedom of speech is one thing, but freedom to think is another. You have to continually abide by the laws of society and that's understood, but you have no idea how limiting this can be for your creative thinking process.

It's the same with bad relationships when they end. Once you're free your heart lights up again and the world is powerless to stop your dreams.

VOLTAIRE
FRENCH AUTHOR

"I disapprove of what you say, but I will defend to the death your right to say it."

Freedom of speech is a truly cherished right, but one you too often take for granted. It is also, I believe, one we don't use enough.

Too often when we have or are given the opportunity to speak out we don't take it and instead are too concerned with what people might think of us.

Well remember, if you don't grasp the opportunity, you could regret it forever.
So make your point proudly.

MAHATMA GANDHI
INDIAN LEADER, MORAL TEACHER AND REFORMER

"The moment the slave resolves that he will no longer be a slave, his fetters fall. He frees himself and shows the way to others. Freedom and slavery are mental states."

How often have you felt imprisoned in your home, business, sport or invironment? Well the chances are you are the victim of your own mental state of well being.

Research shows that when you respect yourself and display your abilities and skills, you receive respect from others and improve your level of well being.

GEORGE ORWELL
ENGLISH NOVELIST

"Freedom is the right to tell people what they do not want to hear."

It takes courage to give people feedback they don't want to hear, but think of the alternative, nothing but praise always.

Coaches in sport have a tough task in growing, educating and moulding their players to reach their full potential.

The critical issue all too often though is the mood, manner, sequence and strategy of their feedback. It's easy to simply criticise, but difficult to give people feedback to learn, grow and develop to succeed.

VOLTAIRE
FRENCH WRITER

"Man is free at the moment he wishes to be."

Nelson Mandela was able, when he was released, to either be totally free in his body and mind or still imprisoned in the past.

He said recently, he chose to be free and focus on the future. They had taken his youth, his ideas, his family, his cause, but not his mind and his body.

You too have the same opportunity.

You can either be trapped in the past or be free in your mind and focus on the future.

ALEXANDER SOLZHENITSYN
RUSSIAN WRITER

"You only have power over people so long as you don't take everything away from them. But when you've robbed a man of everything he's no longer in your power – he's free again."

In other words, a person who takes everything away from someone really creates a new person who is free to change and be the person they want to be.

I know a person who had his wife, children, house, furniture, car and money taken from him by another man but that person is a new man today!

KRIS KRISTOFFERSON
AMERICAN ACTOR AND FOLK SINGER

"Freedom's just another word for nothing left to lose".

In today's economic hardship times many people will lose the lot. It is not pleasant and when it happens you quickly see how supportive your family is and who your friends are.

It's not easy to cope and there are few books to read on the subject. However, what it will do for you is set you free to be the person you want to be. Just ensure you surround yourself with positive, understanding people and focus on your strengths.

DIOGENES
GREEK PHILOSOPHER

"The most beautiful thing in the world is freedom of speech."

It certainly is critical to the success in the world.

When people are supressed they react angrily and rebel against their most basic right of being – to speak.

Whilst this is a beautiful thing, this right must be treated with great sensitivity and diplomacy.

It's easy, for instance, at sporting matches to become too emotional in your thoughts and let out a tirrad of comments that are abusive, obscene and out of order for the people around you.

GEORGE WASHINGTON
FIRST PRESIDENT OF THE UNITED STATES

"Liberty, when it begins to take root, is a plant of rapid growth."

When freedom to build and trade is experienced by a country, it's amazing what growth can be achieved.

This has happened most recently in the United Arab Emarites country of Dubai.

The King, knowing that his countries oil will soon dry up, has given a freedom to his people and their thinking in the way they can create, design and build structures for a new type of oil for the future – tourism.

GEORGE BERNARD SHAW
IRISH DRAMATIST, ESSAYIST AND CRITIC

"Liberty means responsibility. That is why most dread it."

In business you have a great deal of liberty to be who you want to be, do what you want to do, make what you want to make and usually charge what you want to charge.

However, the other equation which is just as powerful is that in business you must be responsible and at the same time acccountable for your actions.

Today, more than ever before, running a business with integrity is the secret ingredient for long term success.

WILLIAM HAZLITT
ENGLISH ESSAYIST

"The love of liberty is the love of others. The love of power is the love of ourselves."

It's interesting how liberty and love are interconnected. You see, you set yourself free when you can love others and you also set yourself free when you love yourself.

Loving yourself however, is often difficult for many people, for they fear they might show over confidence, arrogance or deceit.

However, if you want total freedom you must try to love yourself for who you are and accept your strengths and weaknesses.

ELBERT HUBBARD
AMERICAN WRITER

"Your friend is the man who knows all about you, and still likes you."

A true friend is hard to get, they say, but I say even harder to keep. You see, true friends take you for who you truly are, warts and all.

They like you for who you really are and what you stand for. They give of themselves and often put themselves out for you, even putting themselves under pressure in the process.

They also know more about you than you think and are often prepared to give you insightful feedback.

RALPH WALDO EMERSON
AMERICAN ESSAYIST, POET AND PHILOSOPHER

"The only way to have a friend is to be one."

Being a friend is a great feeling. Have you experienced it lately? It's easy to get lost in your own world, your own affairs, your own work, your own thoughts, but sometimes difficult to have time for others.

To cultivate friends takes time, thought, effort, empathy, planning and understanding the benefits of your actions.

I was once asked, how come you have so many friends, to which I replied, "I make a conscious effort to keep in touch and cultivate them".

KAHLIL GIBRAN
LEBANESE POET, WRITER, ARTIST AND MYSTIC

"Friendship is always a sweet responsibility, never an opportunity."

Being a good friend should be a pleasure, a joy but also a responsibility. It's easy to only be a friend when you want something, but difficult to be a consistent friend without fear or favour.

Friends who only call or contact when they want something are often called "fair weather friends". They only call or contact you when there is an opportunity for them to gain something from their effort.

Watch out for them, they can be toxic!

ROBERT LOUIS STEVENSON
SCOTTISH NOVELIST, POET AND ESSAYIST

"So long as we are loved by others I should say that we are almost indispensable; and no man is useless while he has a friend."

If you ever feel down or depressed try to focus on the fact that you are loved by others and therefore considered worthy or valuable by them.

It is difficult I know to think like this in tough times, but you and you alone must work hard on your own net worth or self esteem to rise up again where you belong.

KATHARINE SUSANNAH PRICHARD
AUSTRALIAN AUTHOR

"Don't sacrifice your life to work and ideals. The most important things in life are human relations. I found that out too late."

It's easy I know to let yourself become consumed by work. Men especially, I observe, need to throw themselves into their work to gain self esteem and personal satisfaction to feel worthy and be recognised by others.

So don't forget to keep balanced and keep in touch with your friends. They are the assets that in the end will provide your best return on investment.

ABRAHAM LINCOLN
FORMER PRESIDENT OF THE UNITED STATES OF AMERICA

"Am I not destroying my enemies when I make friends of them?"

It's interesting isn't it? When you can steal yourself to make friends with people whose behaviour indicates they are in competition with you and are out to make you fail. You actually change them and their attitude towards you.

However, this strategy isn't easy, because first you have to change your attitude toward them.

So, if you want to beat your enemies, work on making friends with them – if you can.

DICK POWELL
AMERICAN ACTOR

"A man who turns his back on his friends soon finds himself facing a very small audience."

Selfishness is a close cousin to loneliness.
If you are you will be.

It's easy with the pace and stress of life to turn your back on friends and focus on your own issues and self importance.

The key to maintaining your network of friends is to maintain your contact with them. Let them know how important they are to you and then they will be there for you when you need them most.

TITUS MACCIUS PLAUTUS
ROMAN POET AND COMIC PLAYWRIGHT

"No man is wise enough by himself."

If you are "an island" as we often hear it said, you can be in big trouble.

Not only will you not learn enough to be wise, but you can become lonely and depressed in your outlook. Cultivating friendships and being amongst people who you like, trust and respect enables you to listen to different points of view and to learn from people and grow.

When you become isolated you can easily break down with too much solitude. Hence criminals being put into solitary confinement.

E.W. HOWE
AMERICAN NOVELIST

"Instead of loving your enemies treat your friends a little better."

Where are your priorities in life? Patronising people you call friends or loving your true friends, unconditionally.

They say your pet, be it a dog or a cat, will love its master unconditionally. This means a total commitment and absolute loyalty no matter what the circumstances.

It is often good to take a "friendship audit" and give yourself a reality check on who are your real friends or just so called friends. Then you can prioritise your life for the better.

ALEXANDRÉ DUMAS
FRENCH NOVELIST

"Friendship consists in forgetting what one gives, and remembering what one receives."

Do you have a set of "friendship scales" in operation, where you continually weigh up or count what you have done for others compared to what they have done for you?

If you do, chances are you are perceived by your friends to be a cold calculating person who is hard to get to know and who is not a "giving person".

If you want to make friends more easily and remain friends with people, throw your "friendship scales" away.

MONTAIGNE
FRENCH ESSAYIST

"He that is a friend to himself, know; he is a friend to all."

Your own positive, loving attitude towards yourself is vital in enabling you to project the same positive, loving attitude to others.

In business especially, it's important to project a positive feeling to your prospects or clients.

You will be surprised how easily people pick up negative or depressed feelings from you by your mood, manner and especially your voice. So check yourself in these tough times and make sure even your phone message is positive and loving of yourself.

MARY ANN EVANS
KNOWN AS GEORGE ELIOT, ENGLISH NOVELIST

"Animals are such agreeable friends – they ask no questions, they pass no criticisms."

No, they just love you for what you are – their friend. In fact, a dog can help you meet friends when you're out walking them. People walking dogs seem to gravitate to one another.

Good friends are like this and enjoy being in your company sharing your thoughts, ideas and opinions.

If you haven't got a dog and you are able to have one, why not buy one and enjoy the experience.

THOMAS MOORE
IRISH POET

"The thread of our life would be dark, heaven knows! If it were not with friendship and love intertwined."

Have you ever noticed another person close by you walking down a street, in a tram, on a train, in a café all serious and quiet.

All of a sudden their mobile phone rings and that same person becomes alive, happy, animated and yes, often very noisy.

In fact these people all of a sudden become actors in the tapestry of day to day life, oblivious to anyone around them.

THOMAS FULLER
ENGLISH DIVINE AND HISTORIAN

"They are rich who have true friends."

I once remember being interested in a friend who was also a very wealthy widow but she was also very difficult to get to know.

We went out to dinner one night and I found the courage to bring up the subject of the future and asked her finally, did she think that she needed to meet someone who was also very wealthy. She immediately answered yes and I replied, "Well I am very wealthy – I have many true friends in life".

SAMUEL TAYLOR COLERIDGE
ENGLISH POET

"Friendship is a sheltering tree."

In 2005 I experienced a devastating personal tragedy and suffered serious shock, anxiety and trauma.

One of the first people to offer help was a friend of over 30 years who put himself out and gave of his time to help me through the tough time.

Then in 2008 the friend was appointed as the General Manager of a resort in Victoria and after renting his home out he suffered shock when his services were terminated without notice. It was then my honour to be his friend and help *him* out.

BENJAMIN DISRAELI
ENGLISH STATEMAN AND AUTHOR

"Friendship is the gift of the gods, and the most precious boon to man."

When your world is crashing around you, when your superannuation is vanishing before your eyes, when you are being retrenched, when your partner is acting strangely, the most precious possession in all the world are your friends.

At these times, reach out and put your friendships to the test. Chances are they will be your shoulder to lean on and your lighthouse to show you a way through the storm.

LAURENCE J. PETER
CANADIAN WRITER

"You can always tell a real friend: when you have made a fool of yourself he doesn't feel you've done a permanent job."

They say the real test of a true friend is the act of forgiveness in a way that has a lighter side to it.

Friends who last through the years do this easily and make light of issues as a way of saving face for you as their real friend. At Christmas John, Ray, John and myself get together to catch up and remember old times, but we each take one another to task in a light hearted way.

Last Christmas the total years we had been friends totalled 155 years.

GRACE CROWELL
AMERICAN POET

"The light of friendship is like the light of phosphorus, even plainest when all around is dark."

During tough times it's easy to fall and lose your way in life. When you get stressed and become distressed you usually make poor decisions and show poor judgement.

It's at times like these that you should seek out the friends that shine like a beacon with strength and attibutes of wisdom. Ask them for help and guidance. Don't be afraid to seek help or be too proud to listen to better ways and better ideas. Remember, when its dark to let the light shine through.

MARY ANN EVANS
KNOWN AS GEORGE ELIOT, ENGLISH NOVELIST

> **"It is never too late to be what you might have been."**

In these tough times it's easy to give up on your goals, stop implementing your plan and throw your hands in the air and change course.

Well just remember, most people give up just before they are about to become successful.

Many people have given up in business just when they were about to solve the problem.

Remember, often the solution to your problem is around the corner to help you be who you wanted to be.

CHARLES FRANKLIN KETTERING
AMERICAN ENGINEER AND INVENTOR

**"I am not interested in the past.
I am interested in the future, for that is
where I expect to spend the rest of my life."**

Do you dwell on the past instead of focussing on the future?

It's easy to let this happen to you and spin your wheels in the mud of memories.

Today more than ever before, it's more motivating to look forward and dream of things you would like to do. It's also healthier and more uplifting to visualise yourself living in the future.

AMBROSE BIERCE
AMERICAN WRITER

"Future – that period of time in which our affairs prosper, our friends are true and our happiness is assured."

It is often said the future is brighter than the past. It's a bit like the sun coming up at dawn and creating another day for achievement.

When you're having a tough time in life, try to think how lucky you are to be alive and to have the friends and family around you that can make you happy.

The main ingredient though is you and your positive belief and effort.

MARCUS AURELIUS
FAMOUS ROMAN EMPEROR AND PHILOSOPHER

"Never let the future disturb you. You will meet it, you have to, with the same weapons of reason which today arm you against the present."

The future often scares people because of the unknown.

In fact you can easily imagine we are all adventurers in the jungle of life, venturing into some unknown world of the future. Well, just think how exciting it would be to be an explorer of the past. Just arm yourself with your skills and talents and take on the challenge.

ABRAHAM LINCOLN
PAST PRESIDENT OF THE UNITED STATES

"The best thing about the future is that it comes only one day at a time."

Some people however, become over whelmed with the thought of the future and either fight it or take flight and hide.

How do you cope with the thought of the future? If you take it one day at a time, you will feel more in control of both it and yourself.

So, if you're becoming over whelmed, remember to focus on one day at a time and put yourself in control.

JOHN MASEFIELD
ENGLISH POET

"To most of us the future seems unsure; but then it always has been, and we who have seen great changes must have great hopes."

I guess you also need great courage to plan and handle what could come your way in the future.

It is inevitable to think and feel some-what unsure of the future, but it is way ahead of the alternative.

So when you are pondering your future, try to be positive and think of the future you want. It just might happen and make you even happier.

AMOS BRONSON ALCOTT
AMERICAN TEACHER AND PHILOSOPHER

"Who loves a garden still his eden keeps, perennial pleasures, plants and wholesome harvest reaps."

There is something special about a garden. In fact it's easy to get lost in time and immerse yourself in your thoughts.

The colours, follage, shapes, sents and sounds of insects buzzing around are aspects of life that are easily missed in the concrete jungle of today's rat race. So do yourself a favour and visit a garden soon and have your breath taken away by its beauty and marvel at mother nature.

MARY HOWITT
ENGLISH AUTHOR

**"Yes, in the poor man's garden grow far
more than herbs and flowers –
kind thoughts, contentments,
peace of mind, and joy for weary hours."**

When you are feeling weary, when you're feeling sad, try and lift your spirits with a shot of scent and inspiration. Gardens of flowers and herbs are amazing tonics for reducing stress and calming yourself.

So if you want to cope better and experience some heartfelt joy in today's world, remember as the famous golfer, Byron Nelson, once said, "Don't forget to smell the roses as you walk through life".

GEORGE R SIMS
ENGLISH POET

"I scorn the doubts and cares that hurt the world and all its mockeries, my only care is now to squirt the ferns among my rockeries. In early youth and later life, I've seen an up and seen a down, and now I have a loving wife to help me peg verbena down.

In peace and quiet pass our days, with nought to vex our craniums, our middle beds are all ablaze with red and white geraniums. Let him who'd have the peace he needs give all his worldly mumming up, then dig a garden, plant the seeds, and watch the product coming up."

Inspiring thoughts for growth.

DOROTHY FRANCES GURNEY
ENGLISH POET

"One is nearer god's heart in a garden, than anywhere else on earth."

Seeing and breathing mother nature at work in a beautiful garden can help you to be more at peace with yourself and the world.

In fact, I experience this amazing feeling at least twice a week at my golf club, Yarra Yarra in Melbourne.

It's one of the most beautiful experiences in the world and walking the fairways with friends like Alan, Graeme, Tim and Kevin and many others, makes you glad to be alive.

THOMAS A EDISON
AMERICAN INVENTOR

"Genius is one per cent inspiration and ninety-nine per cent perspiration."

As my first headmaster at school once said, "If its worth doing, its worth doing well".

It never ceases to amaze me how gifted people with genius seem to find it difficult to understand that they still need to work hard with the right techniques to perform consistently well. But then again it is also said that true genius is often flawed.

Tiger Woods, for example, is a true genius who is flawed but who still works hard trying to perform consistently.

SIMONE DE BEAUVOIR
FRENCH WRITER

"One is not born a genius, one becomes a genius."

It's an interesting question.

From my experience in life, a child can be born with the basic capacity to think as a genius, but it is the environment, the up bringing, the knowledge, the role modelling, the experiences, the discipline and the freedom to think that create the genius.

Therefore, parents have the ability to not only conceive a genius in the making, but also to create a genius in the molding.

WILLIAM HOGARTH
ENGLISH PAINTER AND POLITICAL CARICATURIST

"Genius is nothing but labour and diligence."

There is a well-known golf saying attributed to the famous South African golfer, Gary Player. When asked early in his successful career why he was so successful, Gary Player answered, "The harder I work, the luckier I get".

If ever you wanted the secret ingredient in why people become super successful then this is it.

The famous Australian fast bowler, Glen McGrath is also credited with saying why he became so successful, "I focussed on doing the difficult things that other bowlers don't do in order to become successful".

RALPH WALDO EMERSON
AMERICAN ESSAYIST, POET AND PHILOSOPHER

"To believe your own thought, to believe that what is true for you in your private heart is true for all men – that is genius."

We often call a person a genius when all they have done is believe in themselves and give their idea its best shot.

However, the difference between being a genius or not could simply be the degree of belief in yourself and the degree of "best" that you show in yourself.

Many people in life, business and sport are nearly a genius!

LON G NUNGESSER
WRITER

"You are surrounded by gifts every living moment of every day. Let yourself feel appreciation for their presence in your life and take the time to acknowledge their splendour."

A golfing friend of mine, John Lolas, recently reminded me of a great piece of clever wisdom I heard many years ago. "Yesterday is history, tomorrow is a mystery, but today is a gift – that's why it is called the present!"

When you think of this message it should make you grasp the day.

ELIZABETH BARRETT BROWNING
ENGLISH POET

"Earth's crammed with heaven, and every common bush afire with god."

It's easy to take the ground we walk on and our surrounds for granted.

Life seems to be crammed with roads, train lines, tram lines, footpaths, trams, trains, taxis, cars, motorcycles, push bikes and very, very large, long, dangerous trucks,.

However, it is delightful occassionally to take a walk in a park, in a garden or along the beach. So, why don't you stop and pull the cord of life someday and enjoy nature and perhaps yourself too.

HENRY WADSWORTH LONGFELLOW
AMERICAN POET

"O gift of god! A perfect day, whereon shall no man work but play, whereon it is enough for me not to be doing but to be."

How often do you reward yourself? In fact it's essential to treat yourself to something special as a reward for working hard.

Go out and buy something special to celebrate an achievement.

Take a friend to dinner and simply celebrate you're alive. Book a holiday and pamper yourself for working hard and recharge your batteries. Your light of life will surely shine brighter.

KAHLIL GIBRAN
LEBANESE POET, WRITER, ARTIST AND MYSTIC

"You give but little when you give of your possessions. It is when you give of yourself that you truly give."

We are often judged by others by how much we give of our possessions. The secret of giving, however, is not to be judged by material things, but to give of yourself, unconditionally.

It is then that the real beauty of giving envelopes you and you can experience the total satisfaction it creates.

Just watch their faces and listen to the voices of those you made happy.

RALPH WALDO EMERSON
AMERICAN ESSAYIST, POET AND PHILOSOPHER

"The only gift is a portion of thyself."

How often have you helped someone in need lately?

How often have you called on or telephoned someone to say hi or how are you feeling?

These are the true gifts of greatness that have long lasting memories of thankfulness etched in them.

Too often we can be selfish and not give of ourselves in the spirit of giving. As a result we give up the chance to help others and receive the inner satisfaction of pride.

PIERRE CORNEILLE
FRENCH DRAMATIST

"The manner of giving is worth more than the gift."

It is also said, it is not the gift but the thought that counts. Just the fact that you have thought to give someone something to brighten up their day is more special than the amount of money you have outlayed.

So the next time you are in a quandary about giving a gift to someone special, stop and reflect how important it is just to give without worrying about the value.

A sobering thought in this very commercial world.

GERTRUDE STEIN
AMERICAN WRITER

"You have to know what you want to get. But when you know that, let it take you. And if it seems to take you off the track, don't hold back, because perhaps that is instinctively where you want to be. And if you hold back and try to be always where you have been before, you will go dry."

In other words, once you have set your goals, jump on the train of life and enjoy the ride. Let it take you through a varied countryside on the way to your destination.

HELEN KELLER
DEAF AND BLIND AMERICAN LECTURER, WRITER AND SCHOLAR

"One can never consent to creep when one feels an impulse to soar."

Too often, you would have experienced a feeling of excitement, an adrenaline rush, only to second guess yourself, doubt yourself and go back into your shell.

Well, next time this happens to you think differently, challenge yourself to be brave and live dangerously.

It's only when you want your goals badly enough that you will take flight and soar like an eagle.

LES (LESTER LOUIS) BROWN
JOURNALIST

"Shoot for the moon. Even if you miss it you will land among the stars."

In life, business and sport you often find people or teams, who continually only achieve mediocrity when they really have the ability to achieve significant goals.

Well they also say, "Your attitude effects your altitude". In other words it's how you think that enables your success.

Edward de Bono, the famous lateral thinker, confirms this when he says, "If you aim for success you will survive but if you aim to survive you will fail".

NORMAN VINCENT PEALE
AMERICAN WRITER AND MINISTER

"All successful people have a goal. No one can get anywhere unless he knows where he wants to go and what he wants to be or do."

Many people in life, business and sport, I believe are successful in spite of themselves. They don't set goals to achieve and therefore bump into highlights in their quest for success.

Think of it, would you go on a journey or holiday unless you knew its destination or goal?

Well, it seems many people do and don't care where they arrive as long as they arrive somewhere.

THOMAS CARLYLE
SCOTTISH ESSAYIST, HISTORIAN AND PHILOSOPHER

"A man without a purpose is like a ship without a rudder."

Yes it's true, if you don't have a purpose you will just wander aimlessly throught life and never achieve your full potential.

Not only will you not achieve your full potential, but you will be disappointed with yourself as a person.

So if you want to achieve a feeling of well being, stop, take stock of yourself and set yourself some goals. You will then experience the joy of personal satisfaction and pride in yourself.

KAHIL GIBRAN
LEBANESE WRITER, ARTIST AND MYSTIC

"The significance of a man is not in what he attains, but rather in what he longs to attain."

In 1986 I found myself at the crossroads in life and business. I had achieved my goals and couldn't think what to do next, when a friend at the time gave me the answer.

She said, "Why don't you vere right. Don't turn right and change but just vere right".

In other words, do something similar but not the same and help others along the way with your experience. I did. Wow, what an experience!

KONRAD ADENAUER
GERMAN LAWYER AND STATESMAN

"We're all born under the same sky, but we don't all have the same horizon."

Do you see things the way others see them?

Each one of us, it appears, sets our sights on different goals and thinks differently in how we are going to achieve them.

It's really evident when you get a group of people together and ask each person to describe their goals in life.

It's then that you see the differences in not only how we think, but in what we think we each can achieve.

JOHN F KENNEDY
FORMER PRESIDENT OF THE UNITED STATES

"Once you say you're going to settle for second, that's what happens to you in life, I find."

What's wrong with wanting to be successful? To some people, however, it is not what they feel they can be in life.

To be successful of course, carries with it a responsibility and accountability that can make you both vulnerable and transparent.

You see it is easy to be second in life, business and sport, but it is difficult to be first and the best and this takes a special mindset and self belief.

JOHN WESLEY
ENGLISH EVANGELIST AND FOUNDER OF METHODISM

"Do all the good you can, by all the means you can, in all the ways you can, in all the places you can, at all the times you can, to all the people you can, as long as ever you can."

Do you live by these words?

If you do, chances are that you will be rewarded in many, many ways.

One way that you will be rewarded is in the supreme satisfaction you will feel in doing good and helping other human beings in life.

EILEEN CADDY
CO-FOUNDER OF THE FINDHORN FOUNDATION, SCOTLAND

"Set your sights high, the higher the better. Expect the most wonderful things to happen, not in the future but right now. Realise that nothing is too good. Allow absolutely nothing to hamper you or hold you up in any way."

Do you set your sights high? If not, why not?

I have found that setting your goals low, demotivates you and can even depress you.

However, setting your goals high enables you to dream and activate the endorphins in your brain to enable you to think creatively.

RALPH WALDO EMERSON
AMERICAN POET AND ESSAYIST

"What is a weed? A plant whose virtues have not been discovered."

An interesting comment!

I guess it's all relative. If you're in the botanic gardens, a weed is looked on with scorn and is sprayed or dug out in haste.

However, in the arid waste of the desert, a weed could be looked on as a thing of beauty in a wasted landscape. Therefore, everyone in life is seen differently by people for good or bad reasons and their virtues are often still a mystery waiting to be discovered.

WALTER SAVAGE LANDOR
ENGLISH POET AND WRITER

"Goodness does not more certainly make men happy than happiness makes them good."

Yes, it's true, that you will feel happy when you have done something good to make someone else happy. It's all based on you respecting yourself for being able to display your abilities, skills, energy, thoughtfulness and kindness.

It's then and only then that others really respect you, admire you, promote you, support you and even refer other people to you.

This then completes the circle of influence in building relationships in life, business and sport.

SOCRATES
GREEK PHILOSOPHER

**"Nothing can harm a good man,
either in life or after death."**

As we grow older we see that this is true.
Our reputation is there for all to see,
in life or after death.

Funerals are a great stage for observing the
goodness or greatness of someone.

It's interesting to listen to and observe not only
what people say about someone, but the way in
which they say it. Their reputation can then be
judged by all in attendance and their goodness
embraced, known and remembered forever.

SAPPHO
GREEK LYRIC POET WHO DIED IN 610 BC

"What is beautiful is good, and who is good will soon also be beautiful."

You can easily see pain, depression, disappointment and unhappiness in people's faces.

However, when you have done something good for someone, you feel great, content, proud and satisfied. You're face and eyes change and you take on a relaxed serene beauty.

Doing good deeds for others or doing good things in life generally enables you to take on board the benefits that come from helping others and this is beautiful to see.

G.K. CHESTERTON
ENGLISH AUTHOR

"There is a great man, who makes every man feel small. But the real great man is the man who makes every man feel great."

Yes, I have seen people who instantly put other people down or cut them down to size to push themselves up.

The real issue is that these people lack the self esteem or inner confidence to not have to do this. It's similar with the bully in our society.

Interestingly, these people don't have the self esteem or social skills to not be a bully in the first place.

WILL ROGERS
AMERICAN ACTOR AND HUMORIST

**"It's great to be great,
but it's greater to be human."**

Being human I guess also means being humble.

It's easy when you're excited to feel great and let the greatness in you take over and come out overbearingly in your comments and language.

However, it's the really great people who keep a low profile and let their deeds do the talking.

This emotional behaviour happens to inexperienced people in life until they "get it", or receive feedback by their public or their peers. It's only then that they become great.

VERA BRITTAIN
ENGLISH AUTHOR AND POET

"For the courage of greatness is adventurous and knows not withdrawing, but grasps the nettle danger, with resolute hands, and ever again gathers security from the sting of pain."

In other words, those with greatness and who are adventurous also have great courage and never give up.

In fact, these people gain strength from the experience of pain and never flinch from their goal. They are able to grasp the real issues in their hands and remain focussed on their desired outcome or goal.

These are the really great achievers.

HENRY WADSWORTH LONGFELLOW
AMERICAN POET

"Lives of great men all remind us we can make our lives sublime and, departing leave behind us footprints on the sands of time."

If you want to leave your footprint and a legacy for the future, then you need to understand why this will happen.

It's all to do with how you live your lives and the values you have and display in doing the deeds you do.

It's not compromising on effort and excellence. It's about being who you really are and living your life with integrity and truth.

SIR WINSTON CHURCHILL
ENGLISH STATESMAN AND WAR TIME PRIME MINISTER

"We are all worms, but I do believe that I am a glow-worm."

He believed he was destined to be great and
lived his life as he dreamed and thought
he was — a person of action and achievement,
who would stand out in a time of crisis.
That's when people are truly great.

It's easy to be successful when the climate or
environment is consistent and calm.

However, it's when your world is falling apart that
you have the chance to glow and grow.

ALEXANDER SOLZHENITSYN
RUSSIAN WRITER

"One can build the Empire State Building, discipline the Prussian Army, make a state hierarchy mightier than God, yet fail to overcome the unaccountable superiority of certain human beings."

Perhaps people that feel or need to be superior are so in fact, because deep down they don't think they are superior.

They are really acting like a duck who seems to be gliding majestically on water, when really under the water they are furiously paddling.

As British Prime Minister Maggie Thatcher once said, "If you have to tell people you're powerful, you aren't".

THOMAS CARLYLE
SCOTTISH ESSAYIST, HISTORIAN AND PHILOSOPHER

"The great law of culture is: let each become all that he was created capable of being."

We as parents or grandparents have a great responsibility and accountability today to give our children or grandchildren the best opportunity to be the best they can be.

However, I worry that we often, in our quest to be the best parents, too often create a culture of fear and confinement.

We unthinkingly impose our set of life's values and laws on our children, meaning well, but often imprisoning them.

About the Author

George D Norris
FAICD, FAIM, FAMI, CPM

Australia's most experienced Corporate Coach, Mentor, Facilitator and Speaker.

Coach and Mentor, working with leaders and managers in one-on-one coaching sessions to improve their communication skills and strategic performance.

Meeting Facilitator for retreats, think tanks, business analysis and strategic planning sessions and meetings.

Motivational Speaker specialising in Leadership, Management, Creative Thinking, Change, Communication, Negotiation and Customer Centred Culture.

ORDER

QUOTES & WORDS OF INSPIRATION

	Qty
RRP AU$19.99	.....
Postage within Australia AU$5.00	.....
TOTAL* $_____	*All prices include GST

Name: ....Phone:..
Address: ....
Email: ....

Payment: ❏ Money Order ❏ Cheque ❏ Amex ❏ MasterCard ❏ Visa
Cardholder's Name: ....
Credit Card Number: _ _ _ _ _ _ _ _ _ _ _ _ _ _ _ _

Signature: Expiry Date: _ _ / _ _
Allow 10 days for delivery.
Payment to: Better Bookshop (ABN 14 067 257 390)
              PO Box 12544
              A'Beckett Street, Melbourne, 8006
              Victoria, Australia
              Fax: +61 3 9614 3250
              sales@brolgapublishing.com.au